D0036455

To all my students, whose questions, comments,
and complaints contributed so much to this book.

CONTENTS

PREFACE

This book was written to fill a vacuum. While there are numerous introductory ethics texts on the market today, and more coming out each year, there is surprisingly no up-to-date, introductory social and political philosophy text available. There is Norman Bowie and Robert Simon's *The Individual and the Political Order* (1986), but despite this book's many strengths, it does not contain any discussion of communitarianism, feminism or multiculturalism. There is also Will Kymlicka's *Contemporary Political Philosophy* (1991). This is a fine book in many ways, and it does contain a discussion of communitarianism and feminism. Unfortunately, the complexity of Kymlicka's discussions renders the book too difficult for all but the very best students. It also lacks any discussion of multiculturalism.

So *Contemporary Social and Political Philosophy* is designed to fill the need for an up-to-date, introductory text in social and political philosophy. While this text can have a life of its own in the classroom, like most introductory ethics texts, it can also be profitably used along with anthologies of readings. In fact, two such anthologies have been designed to accompany the text. One, *Justice: Alternative Political Perspectives* second edition (Wadsworth, 1992), provides opposing readings on the major contemporary social and political ideals that are discussed in this new text. The other, *Social and Political Philosophy: Classical Western Texts in Feminist and Multicultural Perspectives* (Wadsworth, 1995), provides the historical roots for the contemporary social and political ideals that we explore here. These ideals are also explicitly discussed in the anthology's contemporary readings, but *Contemporary Social and Political Philosophy* helps students more fully understand and evaluate that discussion. In *Contemporary Social and Political Philosophy*, I also argue for the controversial thesis that *all these contemporary social and political ideals can be reconciled in practice*, which is a really challenging idea for students to discuss and evaluate.

Contemporary Social and Political Philosophy contains simpler and more refined versions of some of the discussions and arguments that I have advanced in my scholarly publication *How to Make People Just* (1988), but the text contains much else besides.

Chapter 1 argues that the central task of political philosophy is to provide a justification for coercive institutions as legitimate authorities. It contends that this justification requires reconciling legitimate authority with our obligation to do what we think is right, and must be given in terms of one or more of the social and political ideals discussed in this text.

Chapter 2 explores the social and political ideal of fairness that has been endorsed by welfare liberals, like John Rawls, applies the ideal to distant peoples and future generations, and considers various challenges that have been raised to it.

Chapter 3 explores the social and political ideal of liberty that has been endorsed by libertarians, like John Hospers, Tibor Machan, and Robert Nozick, and argues that the ideal can be reconciled with the welfare liberal ideal of fairness.

Chapter 4 explores the social and political ideal of equality that has been endorsed by socialists, like C.B. MacPherson, Kai Nielsen and Carol Gould, and considers various objections that have been raised against it.

Chapter 5 explores the social and political ideal of androgyny that has been endorsed by many feminists, like Susan Okin and Ann Ferguson, and considers what practical implications the ideal has for a number of areas, such as family structures, affirmative action, comparable worth and sexual harassment.

Chapter 6 explores the social and political ideal of the common good that has been endorsed by communitarians, like Alasdair MacIntyre and Michael J. Sandel, and considers how objections raised by communitarians to welfare liberalism can be answered.

Chapter 7 explores the social and political ideal of respect for cultural diversity, which virtually everyone endorses, and considers how the ideal should be best interpreted.

Chapter 8 draws on the discussion of social and political ideals in the previous chapters to explore the question of when normal politics, legal protest, civil disobedience, revolutionary action and criminal disobedience are morally permissible.

As one would expect, in writing this book, I have benefited from the help of many different people. In particular, I would like to thank my wife and colleague Janet Kourany, Hugh LaFollette of East Tennessee State University, Robert Paul Wolff of the University of Massachusetts, Larry May of Washington University, and Laurence Thomas of Syracuse University and the following reviewers: Bruce Brower of Tulane University, Wendy Donner of Carleton University, Andrew McLaughlin of Lehman College, and Thomas W. Simon of Illinois State University. I would also like to thank Tammy Goldfeld, philosophy and religion editor at Wadsworth, who encouraged this project from the start, Ruth Cottrell who supervised the production of the book, and John Davenport who is the best proofreader I have ever known.

1

The Central Task of Social and Political Philosophy

The central task of social and political philosophy is to provide a justification for coercive institutions. Coercive institutions range in size from the family to the nation-state and world organizations like the United Nations, with their narrower and broader agendas for action. Yet essentially, they are institutions that at least sometimes employ force or the threat of force to control the behavior of their members to achieve either minimal or wide-ranging goals.[1] To justify such coercive institutions, we need to show that the authorities within these institutions have a right to be obeyed and that their members have a corresponding duty to obey them. In other words, we need to show that these institutions have legitimate authority over their members.

Of course, classical social and political philosophers, like Socrates and Plato, were primarily interested in justifying small city states, like Athens or Sparta. But as larger coercive institutions became both possible and desirable, social and political philosophers sought to justify them. After the seventeenth century, most social and political philosophers focused their attention on justifying the nation-state, whose claim to legitimate authority is restricted by both geography and nationality. But from time to time, and even more frequently in the nineteenth and twentieth centuries, social and political philosophers have sought to justify more wide-ranging coercive institutions, including various forms of world government with more extensive powers than those that are presently exercised by the United Nations.[2] And quite recently, feminist social and political philosophers have raised important challenges to the authority of the family as it is presently constituted.[3]

Obviously, it isn't enough to show that various coercive institutions claim to have legitimate authority over their members or that many or even most of their members accept their claim to such authority. That would only show that these coercive institutions are widely believed to be legitimate authorities, not that they are such. Believing something to be the case never makes it so.

But while coercive institutions that are widely believed to be legitimate authorities may not be such (for example, Nazi Germany), these institutions can still be effective in controlling the behavior of their members, provided that a sufficient number of their members freely acknowledge their claims to be legitimate authorities. Nevertheless, since the control that these coercive institutions maintain over the behavior of their members, at least to some extent, rests on the credibility of their claims to be legitimate authorities, the central task of social and political philosophy is to show how these claims can be justified.

LEGITIMATE AUTHORITIES AND OUR OBLIGATION TO DO WHAT WE THINK IS RIGHT

Unfortunately, any attempt to show that coercive institutions can be legitimate authorities faces a serious problem. The problem is that to recognize any institution as legitimate, and, therefore, as having a right to be obeyed by us seems to conflict with our obligation to do what we think is right. For if any institution has a right to be obeyed by us, we would then have a corresponding obligation to obey because we have been commanded, and such an obligation seemingly conflicts with our obligation to do what we think is right. Of course, we may do what someone commands us to do because we think it is right. For example, we may obey the existing laws against murder and assault because we think they are right. But if we do what someone commands *because* it is commanded, haven't we violated our obligation to do what we think is right? To fulfill our obligation to do what we think is right, don't we have to reject the claims to legitimacy of all coercive institutions and become anarchists of sorts, who may do what coercive institutions require but not because they require it?[4]

Now it might be objected that we don't really have an obligation to do what we think is right, only an obligation to do what is right. So all that needs to be determined is whether it is right for us to obey someone, or some institution, because it is commanded. If so, then, that is what we ought to do, irrespective of whether we happen to think that it is right.

But consider: suppose that after much reflection on the alternatives and their consequences, you decide that you morally ought to do some particular action. Suppose you decide that what you ought to do is to refuse to pay a portion of your federal income taxes that you calculate would be used for excessive military expenditures. Could you be wrong about what you think you morally ought to do? Possibly, but wouldn't that point to some correctable defect in your thinking? Maybe you didn't consider all the alternatives available to you. Obviously, there are other ways that you could protest excessive military expenditures. Or possibly you overlooked some of the effects of your action on other people, such as your family, if, for example, you were to lose your job because of your action. Or maybe your thinking was defective because of some past failure on your part. Maybe you were inattentive when these issues were discussed in the social and political philosophy course you took last year. But if we cannot point to any correctable defect in your thinking, now or in the past, if *you* couldn't have done better in deciding what to do, how could anyone deny that *you* morally ought to refuse to pay a certain portion of your federal income taxes to protest what you take to be excessive military expenditures? If "ought" implies "can," and *you* were unable to see any other alternative as morally better than refusing to pay a portion of your federal taxes, how could it be the case that this is not what *you* ought to do?

It might be objected that although given your abilities and your opportunities you couldn't have come up with a better judgment of what you ought to do, others (maybe experts in the field) might have been able to do so. Naturally, in your defense, if you did your best thinking, you couldn't be morally blamed for doing what you did. For instance, in our example, you really couldn't be morally blamed for refusing to pay a portion of your federal taxes. Still, it might be claimed that it wasn't the morally right thing for you to do. You really shouldn't have refused to pay that portion of your federal taxes.

But what is the force of a moral judgment that is inaccessible to your best judgment? If someone with different abilities or opportunities would have judged differently under the circumstances in which you find yourself, what relevance does that have to what *you* morally ought to do? Again, if there is something that *you* morally ought to do, which presupposes that you are a moral agent capable of moral deliberation, wouldn't it have to be the case that you, using your available opportunities and doing your best thinking, would have come to that realization yourself?

Of course, this is not to suggest that you are infallible—that what you think is right for you to do necessarily is right for you to do. It is only to suggest that if you are a moral agent capable of moral deliberation, any discrepancy between what you think is right for you to do and what is right for you to do must be explained in terms of some kind of past or present failure on your part to follow your best deliberation with regard to the opportunities that are available to you. If it is going to make any sense to say that something is right for you to do, knowledge of that fact must somehow be accessible to you, so that any discrepancy between what you think is right and what is right for you to do must somehow be traceable to a failure on your part to deliberate wisely.[5]

But what then should you do: what is right or what you think is right? Clearly, this is not an option you can see yourself as having. Practically speaking, what is right, as far as you can tell, is what you think is right, all things considered. Only someone else, evaluating your situation from the outside could distinguish between what you think is right for you to do (in our example, refusing to pay a portion of your federal taxes) and what is right for you to do. From your own perspective, having tried your best to come up with what is right, no such distinction exists. Theoretically, of course, you can conceive of the possibility that what you think is right may not be right, but practically you cannot sensibly say that this is what you think is right according to what you regard as your best judgment— refusing to pay a portion of your federal taxes—and this other action—paying all of your federal taxes—is what is really right.[6]

Of course, you will not always have the same degree of confidence about your moral deliberations. Sometimes you will be quite confident that what you think is right is really right. At other times, you will be less so. But as long as you are reasonably confident about your moral deliberation, for you to do anything else than what you think is right would be for you to do what you think is likely to be wrong. Accordingly, it wouldn't make sense, even occasionally, for you to try to get yourself to do what you think is wrong, hoping that on those occasions you may (by sheer chance) be doing what in fact turns out to be right. Surely, the best strategy for you to follow is always to do what, following what you think is your best judgment, you think is right.

Sometimes, however, the choices you face are not so clear. You will find yourself in a dilemma about what to do, such that whatever you decide to do, you will be doing something that is wrong. For example, suppose that you ought to care for your ailing mother and you ought to provide for the needs of your child, but you cannot do both. Normally, in such situations, you should be able to rank the alternatives so that not doing one alternative would be worse than not doing the other. In our example, suppose that your ailing mother is better able to cope without your help than your child is. In this case, the right thing for you to do is to choose the lesser of two evils. Of course, in so acting you would still be doing something that is wrong, or at least prima facie wrong, but clearly you would not be acting as wrongly as you would have if you had selected the other alternative. Selecting the other alternative would be wrong, all things considered.

So compared to what you could have done, your action was right, all things considered.

However, sometimes moral dilemmas are such that you cannot rank the alternatives: failing to choose one alternative is not, all things considered, worse than failing to choose the other, but still you must choose between them. In our example, suppose your mother and your child each desperately needed all your time and help. In such situations, the right thing for you to do, all things considered, is to treat the alternatives as being of equal rank and arbitrarily choose one of them. Under the circumstances, that is the best that you can do, all things considered. Consequently, even when faced with a moral dilemma, the best strategy for you to follow is to use the opportunities available to you, follow your best deliberation, and do what you think is right, all things considered.

Of course, others may think that your moral judgment is in error and that further reflection on your part would lead you to think differently. Accordingly, they may try to get you to do just that by focusing your attention on certain morally relevant considerations. Thus, in our earlier example, others may point out what they believe are more effective ways of protesting an excessive defense budget. Or they may point to some previously unnoticed effects your action will have on others. And if this fails, and you persist in your (erroneous) moral judgment, others may at some point decide to use force to try to stop you from doing what you think is right, all things considered. They may judge that the matter is serious enough that you should not be free to act as you wish on your (erroneous) moral judgment, and they may threaten you with penalties or imprisonment. Yet, notice that even when others in doing what they think is right justifiably attempt to alter your judgment or to forcibly stop you from doing what you think is right, your obligation remains, as always, to do whatever, after attempting to employ your best moral reflection, you think is right. Only now you must also take into account the coercive actions of others in determining what that is.

LEGITIMATE AUTHORITIES AND REFUSING TO REGARD CERTAIN FACTS AS REASONS FOR ACTING

Suppose, then, we grant that you have an obligation to do what you think is right. Does granting this necessarily conflict with recognizing someone as a legitimate authority? Some philosophers have argued that there is no necessary conflict here if it turns out that what you judge is right for you to do is in fact to recognize someone as a legitimate authority.[7] According to these philosophers, your obligation to do what you think is right is basically a procedural obligation.[8] It requires that you follow your best deliberative process of rationally weighing what you take to be competing substantial obligations, and reaching a final decision about what you ought, morally speaking, to do. Rather than being necessarily opposed to your obligation to do what you think is right, your obligation to recognize others to be legitimate authorities is simply one of the competing substantial obligations that you must weigh in fulfilling your procedural obligation to do what you think is right. Hence, so these philosophers maintain, doing what you think is right can be perfectly consistent with recognizing others to be legitimate authorities.

It would seem, therefore, that if your obligation to do what you think is right is a procedural obligation, there would be no necessary conflict with your recognizing a substantial obligation to submit to the claims of coercive institutions to be legitimate authorities. But some critics of legitimate authority, such as Robert Paul Wolff, contend that recognizing an obligation to obey coercive institutions conflicts with an obligation we have to refuse to regard certain sorts of facts as moral reasons for acting.[9] In particular, Wolff contends that we should never consider the fact that something is commanded or the fact that something is the law as a moral reason for acting. Referring to this requirement, Wolff claims that we may do what others tell us to do, but not *because* they have told us to do it.[10] According to Wolff, not only must we engage in moral deliberation and make moral decisions, but we must also refuse to regard certain sorts of facts as moral reasons for acting. By refusing to regard the fact that something is commanded, or the fact that something is the law, as a moral reason for acting, we will thereby reject all claims of coercive institutions to be legitimate authorities.[11]

However, this obligation we have to refuse to regard certain sorts of facts as reasons for acting is subject to two interpretations. One interpretation is that we should refuse to regard certain facts, such as the fact that something is commanded or the fact that something is the law, as ultimate moral reasons for acting, that is, as reasons which are not justified in terms of any other moral reasons for acting, such as the common good. An alternative and stronger interpretation is that we should refuse to regard such facts as even nonultimate moral reasons for acting, that is, as reasons that derive their justification from one or more ultimate moral reasons for acting.[12]

Judging from his remarks in response to critics, Wolff would appear to endorse the first interpretation. He writes,

> I . . . deny that there are, or could be, states which are legitimate in the sense that the validity of their laws constitutes, in itself and independently of considerations of long-run consequences or side-effects, a reason *of any weight at all* for complying with those laws.[13]

And later on in the same article,

> The point is that if a moral agent . . . has already gone through an evaluation of short-run, long-run, direct, and indirect consequences, it would be illogical to say to him, "Now add into your calculations the fact that you have a *prima facie* obligation to obey the law."[14]

In these passages, Wolff is simply denying that we should regard certain sorts of facts as ultimate moral reasons for acting. He is not denying that such facts could serve as nonultimate moral reasons for acting that derive their justification from considerations having to do with short-run and long-run consequences, side effects, and so forth.

However, according to Wolff, defenders of legitimate authority reject the view that the fact that something is the law and the fact that something is commanded are at best *nonultimate* moral reasons for acting. Wolff contends that they hold the mistaken view that such facts are *ultimate* moral reasons for acting. According to Wolff, it is because defenders of legitimate authority hold this mistaken view that the only defensible position open to us is to become anarchists and reject all claims to legitimate authority.

Unfortunately for Wolff's defense of anarchism, defenders of legitimate authority do not hold this mistaken view. Instead, Wolff's own view regarding the nonultimate status of certain moral reasons for acting is actually the view held by most defenders of legitimate authority. For example, contemporary welfare liberals, libertarians, socialists, feminists, and communitarians all deny that facts such as that some action is commanded or that something is required by law are themselves ultimate moral reasons for action.[15] Welfare liberals, like John Rawls, contend that the ultimate moral reason for acknowledging someone as a legitimate authority is justified in terms of fairness while libertarians, like John Hospers and Robert Nozick, contend that it is justified in terms of liberty, and feminists, like Susan Okin, contend that it is justified in terms of androgyny or a gender-free society.[16] By contrast, socialists, like C.B. MacPherson, Kai Nielson, and Carol Gould, contend that the ultimate justification for submitting to someone as a legitimate authority is provided by equality while communitarians, like Alasdair MacIntyre and Michael Sandel, contend that it is provided by the common good. Although obviously disagreeing about the appropriate grounds for and scope of legitimate authority, all of these contemporary philosophers contend that submission to coercive institutions as legitimate authorities can be justified in terms of their respective social and political ideals.

Notice, however, that to claim that submission to coercive institutions as legitimate authorities is justified in terms of one or more of

these ultimate social and political ideals is not to claim that there is anything like a perfect correspondence between what would best promote
these ideals and what legitimate authorities would require. Actually,
the correspondence may be very imperfect indeed, especially when the
parties involved radically disagree about what is right, all things considered. Nevertheless, all that is needed to justify submission to
coercive institutions as legitimate authorities is to show that all other
available alternative courses of actions have far worse consequences
for realizing those ideals.[17] Accordingly, in particular cases, recognizing the claims of coercive institutions may require us to do what we
think is prima facie wrong. Nevertheless, failing to recognize such
claims may undermine the effectiveness of the coercive institutions,
thereby producing worse consequences, leading to an even greater
wrong, all things considered, or so we may think. For example, we may
judge that we should obey some unjust laws while challenging others
because to simultaneously challenge every unjust law could seriously
undermine what are basically just legal systems. Thus, when faced
with dilemmas of this sort, in which submission to the claims of coercive institutions to be legitimate authorities requires submission to
some unjust laws, we must judge that submission in such cases is still
the best way available for realizing our ideals overall.

Despite the general consensus among social and political philosophers concerning the justification of legitimate authority, two
problems remain. First, claiming that legitimate authorities can be justified in terms of some ultimate social and political ideal is one thing,
but providing that justification is another. Thus, it may turn out that
when a justification in terms of some ultimate social and political ideal
like liberty or equality is finally worked out, the fact that something is
commanded or the fact that something is the law will not be shown to
be even a nonultimate moral reason for action, if, for example, the
right political institutions are not yet in place. If so, anarchism will
turn out to be justified after all, at least in certain contexts. Second, the
authorities that are justified by one of these social and political ideals
may not be the same as the authorities justified by another, leaving us
in a quandary as to whom to obey, unless the practical differences
between what these ideals require can be eliminated or compromised.

In succeeding chapters, therefore, we need to examine each of these
social and political ideals—the welfare liberal ideal of fairness, the libertarian ideal of liberty, the socialist ideal of equality, the feminist ideal
of androgyny or a gender-free society, the communitarian ideal of the
common good, and the multicultural ideal of respect for cultural
diversity—to determine, first, whether they support the existence of
legitimate authorities and, second, whether it is possible to eliminate
or compromise the practical differences between what these ideals

require.[18] Not surprisingly, the justification of the very coercive institutions under which we currently live depends upon the outcome of just such an investigation.

Notes

1. Some might think that families are not coercive institutions, but how then do we account for the disciplining of children or the failure of our society to effectively do anything about the large numbers of women who are battered by their husbands when, in fact, many remedies have been suggested?

2. See, for example, Frederick Schuman, *International Politics*, 7th ed. (New York, McGraw-Hill, 1969); Finn Laursen, *Federalism and World Order* (Copenhagen, 1970); Grenville Clark and Louis Sohn, *World Peace Through World Law*, 3rd ed. (Cambridge, MA: Harvard University Press, 1966).

3. See, for example, Janet Kourany, James Sterba, and Rosemarie Tong, *Feminist Philosophies* (Englewood Cliffs, NJ: Prentice Hall, 1991).

4. See Robert Paul Wolff, *In Defense of Anarchism* (New York, Harper & Row, 1970). See also my "The Decline of Wolff's Anarchism," *The Journal of Value Inquiry* (1977): 213–217.

5. The distinction between what you think is right and what is really right works best with objectivist ethical theories, but it even has an interpretation appropriate to those subjectivist ethical theories that distinguish between what is approved of and what would be approved of under certain ideal conditions. See the Introduction to my *Contemporary Ethics* (Englewood Cliffs, NJ: Prentice Hall, 1988).

6. Although with additional information, you may be able to make this distinction about yourself in retrospect.

7. See, for example, Jeffrey Reiman, *In Defense of Political Philosophy* (New York, Harper & Row, 1972), xxiv–xxv; Michael Bayles, "In Defense of Authority," *The Personalist* 52 (1971): 557–558; Robert Ladenson, "Legitimate Authority," *American Philosophical Quarterly* 4 (1972): 337–338.

8. A procedural obligation is an obligation to carry out a certain procedure, like playing a game fairly. By contrast, a substantial obligation is an obligation to do some specific (nonprocedural) action, like keeping one's promises.

9. Wolff, 14, 19, 40.

10. *Ibid.*, 14.

11. Another way of putting Wolff's view is that one has not fully engaged in moral deliberation if one considers the fact that something is commanded or that something is the law as a moral reason for acting.

12. Classifying a moral reason as ultimate or nonultimate leaves open the question of whether it is a prima facie or a conclusive or all-things-considered reason. However, conclusive (prima facie) nonultimate moral reasons would have to derive their justification from conclusive (prima facie) ultimate moral reasons.

13. Robert Paul Wolff, "Reply to Professors Prichard and Smith," *The Journal of Value Inquiry* 7 (1973): 303.

14. *Ibid.*, 305–306.

15. See John Hospers, *Libertarianism* (Los Angeles, Nash, 1971); John Rawls, *A Theory of Justice* (Cambridge, Harvard University Press, 1971); Susan Okin, *Justice, Gender and the Family* (New York, Basic, 1989); Kai Nielson, *Equality and Liberty* (Totowa, NJ: Rowman and Littlefield, 1985); Alasdair MacIntyre, *After Virtue* (Notre Dame, IN: University of Notre Dame Press, 1981). In replying to his critics (*In Defense of Anarchism* expanded edition (New York, 1976, 110ff), Wolff has accused defenders of legitimate authority of failing to consistently hold to the view that authority can only be derivatively justified in terms of other moral reasons for action. He claims that defenders of legitimate authority have frequently slipped into regarding the fact that someone commanded a person to do something or the fact that something is required by the law as itself an ultimate moral reason for action. Yet even if this were true (and the evidence is at least mixed), it would not provide any reason at all for accepting anarchism. It would only show that defenders of legitimate authority are sometimes inconsistent. It would not show that legitimate authority could not in fact be derivatively justified in terms of ultimate moral reasons for actions.

16. For a definition of androgyny and a gender-free society, see Chapter 5.

17. For further discussion, see Joseph Raz, *The Morality of Freedom* (Oxford, Oxford University Press, 1986), Part I.

18. One might wonder why the ideal of a society free from racism is not another social and political ideal worth examining in a text such as this. The reason is that the social and political ideals that are considered in the text are ideals for which contemporary philosophers have offered plausible arguments *both* for and against, whereas nothing similar holds for the ideal of a society free from racism. This is because there are not any plausible arguments for racism. Nevertheless, it is still important to assess the social and political ideals that are considered in the text to determine to what degree they help to overcome the many forms of racism that are still found in contemporary societies.

2

Welfare Liberalism: The Ideal of Fairness

Every social and political view has some place for an ideal of fairness. According to some social and political views, fairness is only a formal ideal, requiring that like cases be treated alike. In such views, everything depends on the criteria used to determine like cases. For example, without offending against this formal ideal of fairness, African Americans could be given fewer rights than whites, and women could be given fewer rights than men simply by using racist and sexist criteria to define what are like cases. According to other social and political views, fairness is a procedural ideal, requiring that cases be decided according to established rules. In such views, everything depends on what rules are established. For example, in a criminal justice system, certain rules of evidence and due process are likely to achieve just results while others that automatically favor those with wealth and status are not. Yet both sets of rules, if established and adhered to, would be procedurally fair.

But in more defensible social and political views, the ideal of fairness is not just a formal or procedural ideal, but also a substantive one that requires certain fundamental rights and duties. Welfare liberalism, however, is the only contemporary social and political view of this sort that takes an ideal of fairness as its core requirement.[1] It is the view endorsed by the left wing of the Democratic party in the United States whose leaders have been Jesse Jackson and Ted Kennedy. Its fundamental rights and duties have been defended by John Rawls and other contemporary social and political philosophers as the rights and duties that people would agree to under certain conditions.[2] It is this substantive ideal of fairness that will be the focus of this chapter.

THE IDEAL OF FAIRNESS AND THE ORIGINAL POSITION

To begin, this substantive ideal of fairness does not say that the fundamental rights and duties that people should have are those to which they actually agree. In fact, the rights and duties to which people actually agree might not be fair at all. For example, people might agree to a certain system of fundamental rights and duties only because they are forced to do so or because their only alternative is certain death, as in Nazi concentration camps. So actual agreement is not sufficient, nor is it even necessary according to this ideal; what is necessary and sufficient is that people *would agree* to such rights and duties under certain ideal conditions.

But what are the conditions required for reaching such an agreement? According to John Rawls, this ideal of fairness requires that we discount certain knowledge about ourselves in order to reach fair agreements.[3] A good example of what is at issue here is the practice of withholding information from juries. As we know, judges sometimes refuse to allow juries to hear certain testimony. The rationale behind this practice is that certain information is highly prejudicial or irrelevant to the case at hand. The hope is that without this information, juries will be more likely to reach fair verdicts. Similarly, when prejudicial or irrelevant information is blurted out in the courtroom, intentionally or unintentionally, judges will usually instruct juries to discount that information to increase the likelihood that juries will reach fair verdicts. Of course, whether judges and juries in fact carry out their responsibilities in this regard is beside the point. What is crucial is that it is recognized in these contexts that fairness demands that we discount certain information in order to achieve fair results.

Rawls's ideal of fairness can be seen as simply a generalization of this practice. The ideal maintains that if we are to achieve a fair system of rights and duties in general, then we must discount certain information about ourselves when choosing our system of rights and duties. In particular, the ideal maintains that we must discount our knowledge of whether we are rich or poor, talented or untalented, male or female when choosing our system of rights and duties. In addition, in order to ensure that our choices are valid for distant peoples (that is, people who live in other societies) and future generations, as well as for the members of our own society, we also must discount information concerning the society, and even the generation to which we belong. For without discounting such information, we could unfairly favor our own society over other societies, or our own generation over other generations.[4] In general, this ideal of fairness requires that we should choose as though we were standing behind an imaginary "veil of ignorance" with respect to most particular facts about ourselves—anything that would bias our choice or stand in the way of unanimous agreement. Rawls calls this fair-choice situation *the original position* because it is the position we should start from when determining what fundamental rights and duties people should have.

But what rights and duties would be chosen in the original position? Rawls argues that a system of rights and duties that maximizes benefit to the least advantaged position would be chosen.[5] This is called the *maximin* view because it would *maximize* benefit to those who have the *min*imum. Rawls argues that persons in the original position would favor the maximin view because the choice of a system of rights and duties for a society is of utmost importance, and persons in the original position are choosing in ignorance of the probabilities of their occupying any particular place in society (for example, the probability of their being rich or poor, talented or untalented). In such circumstances, Rawls claims, it is rational to follow the maximin view.

To better understand what this maximin view requires, consider a society with just three individuals A, B, and C each facing the following alternatives:

| | Individuals | | | |
Alternatives	A	B	C	Average
I	4	7	12	7 2/3
II	3	8	14	8 1/3
III	5	6	8	6 1/3

Imagine that the numbers represent comparable benefits or utilities to the three members of this society. Now the maximin view would favor alternative III, because only that alternative maximizes the benefit to the least advantaged member of this society, despite the fact that the other two alternatives offer a higher average expected benefit or utility to each member of the society. According to the maximin view, when making important choices in (imagined) ignorance of how those choices will affect one personally, it is most rational to maximize the benefit to the least advantaged individual in order to guard against the possibility that this individual will turn out to be oneself.

Others, however, most notably John Harsanyi, have argued that persons in the original position would reject the maximin view in favor of a system of rights and duties that maximizes average expected benefit or utility.[6] This is called the *utilitarian* view because it requires that we maximize average expected benefit or utility over the relevant group. In our example, the utilitarian view would favor alternative II because that alternative provides the highest average expected benefit or utility. According to the utilitarian view, when making important choices in (imagined) ignorance of how those choices will affect one personally, it is most rational to first assign an equal probability to one's occupying each particular position and then select the alternative with the highest average expected benefit or utility.

Still others have argued for rejecting both the maximin and utilitarian views in favor of a system of rights and duties that strikes a reasonable compromise between the more advantaged and the less advantaged.[7] This can be called the *compromise* view. In our example, it would favor the choice of alternative I, assuming that its lower minimum and lower maximum benefits can be shown to be acceptable to the less advantaged, and the more advantaged, respectively. According to the compromise view, when making important choices in (imagined) ignorance of how those choices will affect one personally, it is most rational to compromise the interests of the less advantaged and the more advantaged.

Not surprisingly, there has been considerable debate over which of these views is most defensible.[8] In this debate, however, it is usually assumed that the maximin, utilitarian, and compromise views will always lead to different alternatives, as in our example. So it is assumed that in the original position the system of rights and duties that maximizes benefit to the least advantaged individual will be different from the system that maximizes average expected benefit or utility and also different from the system that strikes a reasonable compromise between the more advantaged and the less advantaged individuals. But this assumption need not obtain.

Consider the following example with individuals A through T and alternatives x, y, and z.

	Individuals	Average
Alternatives	A B C D E F G H I J K L M N O P Q R S T	
x	3 3 3 3 3 3 3 3 3 3 3 3 3 3 3 3 3 4 4 5	3 1/5
y	1 1 1 1 1 1 1 1 1 1 1 1 3 3 3 3 4 5 7 8	2 2/5
z	0 0 0 0 0 0 1 1 1 1 1 3 3 4 6 6 7 7 8 9	2 9/10
	Expected Benefits	

In this example, the alternative that best satisfies the requirements of the maximin, utilitarian, and compromise views is the same: alternative x. This is because it alone provides the highest minimum, thus satisfying the maximin view; and it provides the highest average expected utility, thus satisfying the utilitarian view; and assuming that 3 units of benefit is the minimally acceptable benefit to those in the least advantaged position, this alternative also strikes a reasonable compromise between the more advantaged and the less advantaged, thus satisfying the compromise view.

What this example shows is that, at least theoretically, the assumption that the maximin, utilitarian, and compromise views will lead to different alternatives need not obtain. Furthermore, once the imaginary veil of ignorance in the original position is extended to include distant peoples and future generations in addition to the members of our own society, the assumption that the maximin, utilitarian, and compromise views will lead to different alternatives would not hold in practice either. This is because once the veil of ignorance in the original position is extended to distant peoples and future generations as well as the members of our own society then in order to guarantee *everyone* an acceptable minimum, both the maximin and compromise views would favor a set of rights and duties that provides a minimum that is lower than the one that would otherwise be favored for the members of an affluent society like our own, taken in isolation. This is because only a lower minimum could be guaranteed to everybody. The utilitarian view would also have to favor the same sort of minimum, but it would do so as the best way of maximizing average expected utility among so many people. This is because the inequalities that the utilitarian view might theoretically justify (as in our earlier example) would not in fact be justified, given the need to provide an acceptable minimum for so many people. Consequently, once the imaginary veil of ignorance is extended to cover distant peoples and future generations, as well as the members of our own society, then the maximin, utilitarian, and compromise views would all be seen to favor the choice of the same social minimum.

A BASIC-NEEDS MINIMUM

Now it is possible to specify the social minimum that would be favored behind the imaginary veil of ignorance in terms of the satisfaction of a person's basic needs. A person's basic needs are those that must be satisfied in order not to seriously endanger a person's mental or physical well-being. Needs in general, if not satisfied, lead to lacks and deficiencies with respect to various standards. Basic needs, if not satisfied, lead to significant lacks and deficiencies with respect to a standard of mental and physical well-being. A person's needs for food, shelter, medical care, protection, companionship, and self-development are, at least in part, needs of this sort. Obviously, societies vary in their ability to satisfy the basic needs of their members, but the needs themselves would vary only to the degree that there is a corresponding variation in what constitutes health and sanity in different societies. Consequently, requiring the satisfaction of a person's basic needs is a fairly determinate way of specifying the minimum of goods and resources that each person has a right to receive.

It still seems likely, nevertheless, that an acceptable minimum should vary over time and among societies, at least to some degree. For example, it could be argued that today a car is almost a necessity in the typical North American household, a fact that was not true sixty years ago nor true today in most other areas of the world. Happily, a basic-needs approach to specifying an acceptable minimum can account for such variation without introducing any variation into the definition of the basic needs themselves. Instead, variation enters into the cost of satisfying these needs at different times and in different societies. This is because in the same society at different times, and in different societies at the same time, the normal costs of satisfying a person's basic needs can and do vary considerably.

These variations are due in large part to the different ways in which the most readily available means for satisfying basic needs are produced. In more affluent societies, the most readily available means for satisfying a person's basic needs are usually processed so as to satisfy nonbasic needs at the same time as they satisfy basic needs (for example, multicolored breakfast cereals with "free" base-ball cards included).[9] This is done to make the means more attractive to persons in higher income brackets who can easily afford the extra cost. As a result, the most readily available means for satisfying basic needs are much more costly in more affluent societies than in less affluent societies. This occurs most obviously with respect to the most readily available means for satisfying basic needs for food, shelter, and transportation, which are highly processed in more affluent societies, but it also occurs with respect to the most readily available means for satisfying basic needs for companionship, self-esteem, and self-development. In fact, someone in more affluent societies cannot normally satisfy even these latter needs without par-ticipating in at least some relatively costly educational and social development practices (for example, twelve years of education plus additional job training).

Accordingly, there will be considerable variation in the normal costs of satisfying a person's basic needs as a society becomes more affluent over time, and considerable variation at the same time in societies at different levels of affluence. There will even be variation between indi-viduals in the same society at the same time. For example, the normal costs of meeting the basic self-development and health-care needs of those who are disabled or have special health problems will be greater than those of the average member of the society.

Difficult cases will also arise in which it will not be possible to sat-isfy everyone's basic needs. Given the technological advances in modern medicine, meeting the basic needs of all those with special health-care problems can conflict with the satisfaction of the basic needs of others. For example, heart transplants are estimated to cost between $80,000 to $150,000. Obviously, then, to provide a heart transplant to everyone who needs one, even assuming a sufficient number of donors, would conflict with meeting other people's basic needs.

To resolve such conflicts, it is necessary to return to the moral framework used to justify the basic-needs approach in the first place, that is, to persons choosing in the original position from behind an imaginary veil of ignorance. From this perspective, persons whose basic needs would normally be met with less cost would have priority over those whose basic needs would usually be more costly to meet. Thus, meeting the basic needs of those without costly special health problems would have priority over meeting the basic needs of those with costly problems, as in the preceding example.

In sum, a basic-needs approach to specifying an acceptable minimum would guarantee people the goods and resources necessary to meet at least the normal costs of satisfying their basic needs in the society in which they live. Thus, once the imaginary veil of ignorance is extended to include distant peoples and future generations, persons in the original position would choose to have just such a minimum guaranteed to everyone. This is the fundamental requirement of welfare liberalism.

It should be noted that in *Wyman v. James* (1971), one of the few U.S. Supreme Court decisions pertaining to a guaranteed minimum, the majority of the Court did not recognize any constitutional right to a guaranteed minimum, only a right that is conditional upon the willingness of particular states to provide that minimum. Obviously, the right to a guaranteed minimum that is defended by welfare liberals is much stronger than this, and it would limit the type of constraints, such as home visitations, that states could impose on the provision of that minimum.

A Basic-Needs Minimum for Distant Peoples and Future Generations

At present, there is probably a sufficient worldwide supply of goods and resources to meet the normal costs of satisfying the basic nutritional needs of all existing persons. According to former U.S. Secretary of Agriculture Bob Bergland,

> For the past 20 years, if the available world food supply had been evenly divided and distributed, each person would have received more than the minimum number of calories.[10]

Other authorities have made similar assessments of the available world food supply.

Needless to say, the adoption of a policy of supporting a right to welfare for all existing persons would necessitate significant changes, especially in developed countries. For example, the large percentage of the U.S. population whose food consumption clearly exceeds even an adequately adjusted poverty index would have to substantially alter their eating habits. In particular, they would have to reduce their consumption of beef and pork in order to make more grain available for direct human consumption. Presently, the amount of grain fed to American livestock annually (64 percent of the total U.S. grain crop) is as much as all the people of China and India, with their much larger populations, eat in a year. Thus, the satisfaction of at least some of the nonbasic needs of the more advantaged in developed societies would have to be forgone, leading to greater equality, so that the basic nutritional needs of all existing persons in developing and underdeveloped societies could be met.

Of course, meeting the long-term basic nutritional needs of these societies, will require other kinds of aid including appropriate technology and training and the removal of trade barriers favoring developed societies.[11] Furthermore, to raise the standard of living in developing and underdeveloped countries will require substantial increases in the consumption of energy and other resources. But such an increase would have to be matched by a substantial decrease in the consumption of these goods in developed countries; otherwise, global ecological disaster would result from increased global warming, ozone depletion, and acid rain, lowering virtually everyone's standard of living.[12]

In addition, once the basic nutritional needs of future generations are also taken into account, the satisfaction of the nonbasic needs of the more advantaged in developed countries would have to be further restricted in order to preserve the fertility of cropland and other food-related natural resources for the use of future generations. Obviously, the only assured way to guarantee the energy and resources necessary for the satisfaction of the basic needs of future generations is to set aside resources that would otherwise be used to satisfy the nonbasic needs of existing generations.

Once basic needs other than nutritional needs are taken into account as well, still further restrictions would be required. For example, it has been estimated that presently a North American uses fifty times more resources than an Indian. This means that in terms of resource consumption the North American continent's population is the equivalent of 12.5 billion Indians.[13] So unless we assume that basic resources, such as arable land, iron, coal, oil, and so forth are in unlimited supply, then this unequal consumption would have to be radically altered if the basic needs of distant peoples and future generations are to be met.[14] And eventually the practice of utilizing increasingly more efficient means of satisfying people's basic needs in developed societies would have the effect of equalizing the normal costs of meeting people's basic needs across societies.

Nevertheless, while the demands that satisfying a basic-needs minimum place on those in developed affluent societies are obviously quite severe, they are not unconditional. Those in developing and underdeveloped societies are under a corresponding obligation to do what they can to meet their own basic needs, for example, by bringing all arable land under optimal cultivation and by controlling population growth. However, we should not be unreasonable in judging what particular developing and underdeveloped societies have managed to accomplish in this regard. In the final analysis, such societies should be judged on the basis of what they have managed to accomplish given the options open to them. For example, developing and underdeveloped societies today do not have the option, which western European societies had during most of the last two centuries, of exporting their excess population to sparsely populated and resource-rich continents. In this and other respects, developing and underdeveloped societies today lack many of the options western European societies were able to utilize in the course of their economic and social development. Consequently, in judging what developing and underdeveloped societies have managed to accomplish we must take into account the options that they actually have available to them in their particular circumstances.

CHALLENGES TO THE IDEAL OF FAIRNESS

So far it has been argued that the substantial ideal of fairness represented by the choice of persons in the original position would favor a social minimum specified in terms of the satisfaction of people's basic needs. However, the imaginary choice situation of the original position has been subject to a number of important challenges. All of these challenges are directed at the very idea of the original position.

The Challenge from the Nature of Hypothetical Agreements

In an early challenge to the very idea of the original position, Ronald Dworkin argues that hypothetical agreements, such as the agreement persons would make in the original position, do not (unlike actual agreements) provide independent arguments for the fairness of those agreements.[15] For example, suppose yesterday if you had offered me $100 for a painting I owned, I *would have accepted* your offer because I did not know the value of a painting. Dworkin argues that such hypothetical acceptance in no way shows that it would be fair to force me to sell the painting to you today for $100 now that I have discovered it to be more valuable. Accordingly, Dworkin holds that the fact that persons would hypothetically agree to do something in the original position does not provide an independent argument for abiding by that agreement in everyday life.

But while it seems correct to argue that hypothetical agreement in the painting case does not support a demand that I presently sell you the painting for $100, it is not clear how this undermines the relevance of the hypothetical agreement that emerges from the original position. For surely a defender of the original position need not endorse the view that *all* hypothetical agreements are morally binding. Nor could Dworkin reasonably argue that his example supports the conclusion that *no* hypothetical agreements are morally binding. Because if that were the case, we could argue from the fact that *some* actual agreements are not binding (such as an agreement to commit murder) to the conclusion that *no* actual agreement is morally binding, which, of course, is absurd. Consequently, Dworkin would have to provide some further argument to show that the specific agreement that would result from the original position is not morally binding. He can't derive that conclusion simply from the premise that some hypothetical agreements (for example, the one concerning the picture) are not morally binding.

The Challenge from the Nature of Persons

Another challenge to the very idea of the original position is that its veil of ignorance requires us to view persons as stripped of their rightful natural and social assets such as their native skills and family wealth. Now Rawls does say that the veil of ignorance is designed to reflect the judgment that people do not deserve their natural assets or initial social status. Yet this judgment, when correctly interpreted, does not imply that a person's natural or initial social assets are undeserved, but only that the notion of desert does not apply to them because people could not have done anything to merit their natural and initial social assets. Yet Rawls also claims that in the original position, natural assets and initial social assets are regarded, in effect, as common assets.[16] Thus, persons in the original position might even choose to require people to donate their surplus kidneys to those in need. For this reason, Robert Nozick and Michael J. Sandel have claimed that Rawls's substantive ideal of fairness does not take seriously the distinction between persons because it severely restricts people's rights to use their own natural and social assets.[17]

In defense of Rawls, it can be argued that he is simply addressing a question every moral philosopher must address: What constraints, if any, should apply to people's use of their natural and social assets in the pursuit of their own welfare? For example, should people be able to use such assets in pursuit of their own welfare, regardless of the consequences to others? Egoists, of course, would say that they should, but most moral philosophers would disagree. Even libertarians, like Nozick, who prize the ideal of liberty, would object to such unconstrained use of people's natural and social assets. For Nozick, people's use of their natural and social assets is constrained by the moral requirement that they not interfere with or harm other people, or at least that they not do so without paying compensation. For others, particularly welfare liberals, the use of people's natural and social assets would be constrained not only when it interferes with or harms other people, but also when such use fails to benefit others in fundamental ways—for example, by not providing them with a basic-needs minimum.

So the charge that the ideal of fairness does not take seriously the distinction between persons ultimately comes down to the claim that although some constraints are morally justified, the ideal puts *too many* constraints on the use of a person's natural and social assets (for example, by providing a basic-needs minimum rather than simply a right of noninterference). But to make this charge stick, critics of this ideal need to provide an acceptable argument that only a more limited number of constraints on the use of natural and social assets are morally justified. Whether they can provide such an argument remains to be seen. We will consider one such attempt in Chapter 3.

A related objection raised by Elizabeth Wolgast, among others, interprets the original position as making a metaphysical claim about our essential nature.[18] Since the original position requires that we imagine ourselves to be ignorant of virtually all of our particular traits, this is seen to imply the view that none of those traits are essential to who we are. So interpreted, the original position would commit us to a form of social atomism, according to which each person can be adequately individuated and understood apart from his or her social relationships to other people. In fact, since the veil of ignorance extends beyond socially acquired traits to native intelligence, race, and sex, these traits too would be seen as inessential to who we are. But surely, Wolgast contends, such a view of our essential nature is radically contestable.

Fortunately, the original position need not be interpreted as implying anything about our essential nature. Rather, it simply expresses a stance concerning which traits we should take into account when choosing a system of rights and duties that should govern ourselves and others. To secure a fair choice, we are required to imagine ourselves to be ignorant of most of our particular traits. But this imagined ignorance implies nothing about what traits individuals essentially possess. Virtually any answer to the question of what traits individuals essentially possess is compatible with the ideal of fairness represented by the original position.

The Challenge from the Knowledge Restrictions on the Original Position

In still another challenge to the idea of the original position, Richard Miller argues that if the original position is specified to include the knowledge of the general facts of class conflict, then, no agreement would be reached.[19] Miller claims that if persons in the original position are aware of the facts of class conflict, they will know that members of different classes have diametrically opposed interests and needs, with the consequence that social arrangements that are acceptable to members of one class, say the rich, propertied capitalist class, will be quite unacceptable to members of an opposing class, in this case the poor, relatively propertyless proletariat class. For this reason, Miller claims that if persons know that conflicts between opposing classes cannot be resolved without leaving members of one or the other group extremely dissatisfied with the result, they will not be able to reach agreement in the original position.

To understand the force of Miller's critique, it is necessary to understand the various ways in which people's needs and interests can be related in a society. One possibility is that the needs and interests of different members of a society are in fact perfectly complementary. If that were the case, there would be little difficulty in designing a social arrangement that was acceptable to every member. Nor would the original position be needed to design a fair solution. In such a society, no conflicts would arise as long as each person acted in his or her overall self-interest.

A second possibility is that the needs and interests of different members of a society are in moderate conflict. In his use of the original position, Rawls actually limits himself to a consideration of social conditions where only moderate conflict obtains. For such conditions it seems clear that the original position can be usefully employed to design a fair social arrangement. In such a society the more talented members would be motivated to contribute sufficiently to support a social minimum, and the less talented would also be motivated to contribute sufficiently to reduce the burden on the more talented members. Consequently, persons in the original position would know that the members of such a society when aided by a minimal enforcement system would be able to abide by the requirements that would be chosen.

A third possibility is that the needs and interests of the different members of a society are in extreme conflict, and that the conflict has the form of what Marx calls "class conflict." Let us consider the case in which the opposing classes are the rich, propertied capitalist class and the poor, relatively propertyless proletariat class. No doubt persons in the original position would know that in such a society compliance with almost any principles of conflict resolution could be achieved only by means of a stringent enforcement system. But why should that fact keep them from choosing any principles of social cooperation whatsoever? Surely, persons in the original position would still have reason to provide for the basic needs of the members of the poor, relatively propertyless proletariat class because they may turn out to be in that class, and thus would be inclined to favor a basic-needs minimum.

Of course, members of the capitalist class who have developed special needs for wealth and power could claim that they would suffer acutely in any transition to a society with a basic-needs minimum. Yet persons in the original position, imagining themselves to be ignorant of whether they belong to the capitalist or the proletariat class, would have grounds to discount such considerations in deciding upon principles of social cooperation. They would realize that members of the capitalist class are not "compelled" to pursue their interest by depriving the members of the proletariat class of an acceptable minimum of social goods. They act as they do, depriving others of an acceptable social minimum, simply to acquire more social goods for themselves. Unlike members of the proletariat class, the members of the capitalist class could be reasonably expected to act otherwise. Persons in the original position, therefore, have no more reason to temper the sacrifice to be imposed on the members of the capitalist class than they would have to temper the sacrifice to be imposed on criminals who have grown accustomed to the benefits provided by their ill-gotten goods. Accordingly, requiring a significant sacrifice from the members of the capitalist class would be necessary to restore to the members of the proletariat class the benefits of the social minimum that would be agreed to in the original position.

Someone might object to the analogy between criminals and capitalists on the grounds that while the actions of criminals are usually condemned by the conventional standards of their society, the actions of capitalists usually find approval from those same standards. How can we blame capitalists for acting in accord with the conventional standards of their society?

Despite the fact that capitalist exploitation, which denies people a basic-needs minimum, differs from criminal activity in that it is supported by conventional standards, capitalists who engage in such exploitation still cannot escape blame for acting immorally for two basic reasons. First, capitalists have alternatives to pursuing their own advantage to the limit allowed by conventional standards. For while some capitalists are pursuing their own advantage, others are attempting to restrict at least some of the rights normally enjoyed by capitalists under those standards by supporting welfare and other social programs, and still others are trying to effect a drastic reform, even a revolutionary change, in those rights.

Second, although supported by conventional standards, capitalist exploitation, which denies people a basic-needs minimum, is contrary to the moral presuppositions of capitalist society, in the same manner that "separate but equal education," although supported by state and local laws, was contrary to the supreme law of the land contained in the equal protection clause of the Fourteenth Amendment. This is because the moral presuppositions of capitalist society as expressed by the ideal of fairness (or as we shall see, even by the ideal of liberty) can be shown to be contrary to capitalist exploitation. For these reasons, capitalists cannot escape blame for acting immorally if they deny people their rights required by these ideals, despite the existence of supportive conventional standards.

Of course, it goes without saying that many capitalists would be reluctant to accept the practical requirements of their own social and political ideals. Many would be strongly tempted to endorse uncritically the justification for their favored status provided by the conventional standards of their society. But this is exactly what they cannot do if they are to avoid blame for acting immorally. For all of us when faced with choices that have social impact are required to evaluate critically the alternatives open to us in light of our social and political ideals; and the greater the social impact our choices will have, the greater is our responsibility for performing this critical evaluation well. Since even a cursory examination of the alternatives open to capitalists in our times gives rise to serious doubts about the morality of the conventional standards supporting capitalist exploitation, capitalists who continue to engage in such exploitation surely will not be able to escape blame. Consequently, persons in the original position would have no reason to temper the sacrifice to be imposed on the members of the capitalist class in the transition to a basic-needs minimum.

Yet it is important to note that even though the assumption of class conflict would not lead persons in the original position to temper the sacrifice to be imposed on the members of the capitalist class, the assumption of moderate conflict would lead to somewhat different results. Under the assumption of class conflict, persons in the original position would tend to justify drastic measures, even violent revolution, to bring into existence a society with a basic-needs minimum, together with a stringent enforcement system to preserve such a society by preventing capitalists from lapsing back into exploitative ways.

On the other hand, under the assumption of moderate conflict, persons in the original position would tend to justify only less drastic means both with regard to bringing into existence and preserving such a society. Accordingly, the question of which type of conflict characterizes a particular society is of considerable practical moral significance. But whichever obtains, persons in the original position would still be able to use the information to arrive at morally acceptable results.[20]

In conclusion, none of these challenges to the very idea of the original position has been shown to be successful. Rather what has been shown is that the ideal of fairness captured by the original position supports a social minimum specified in terms of the satisfaction of a person's basic needs.

LEGITIMATE AUTHORITIES AND THE IDEAL OF FAIRNESS

The question of whether the welfare liberal's ideal of fairness can justify coercive institutions as legitimate authorities remains. At first glance, when one considers the degree of redistribution that would be necessary to achieve a basic-needs minimum within our own society and in the world at large, it is hard to see how coercive institutions could be avoided. Of course, the degree to which coercive institutions would be required would depend on the level and type of opposition that existed to achieving a basic-needs minimum. Other things being equal, the greater the opposition to securing and maintaining such a social minimum, the greater the need for coercive institutions.

Nevertheless, whether and to what degree coercive institutions can be justified depends on more than the level and type of opposition to achieving an acceptable social minimum. It also depends on the relationship between the welfare liberal's ideal of fairness with its basic-needs minimum and alternative social and political ideals and their practical requirements. If alternative social and political ideals have quite different practical requirements, and we cannot reasonably establish which ideal is morally preferable, then it isn't clear how we would be able to justify any particular institutional arrangements, coercive or otherwise. We can only hope that our investigations of other social and political ideals in subsequent chapters will somehow resolve this problem.

Notes

1. Socialism and communitarianism, which we will discuss in Chapters 4 and 6, also interpret fairness to be a substantial ideal, but neither takes it to be its core requirement.

2. See, for example, John Rawls, *A Theory of Justice* (Cambridge, Harvard University Press, 1971); Charles Beitz, *Justice and International Relations*,

(Princeton: Princeton University Press, 1985); James P. Sterba, *The Demands of Justice* (Notre Dame, IN: University of Notre Dame Press, 1980). Following Rawls, many contemporary social and political philosophers have associated the welfare liberal ideal of fairness with the social contract theories of Locke, Rousseau, and Kant, but not with the social contract theory of Hobbes. For a discussion of a contemporary defense of the Hobbesian view, see my *How to Make People Just* (Totowa, NJ: Rowman & Littlefield, 1988), Chapter 11.

3. Rawls, Chapter 2.

4. Rawls does not argue for discounting information concerning the society and generation to which one belongs, but for reasons why this information should be discounted, see my *How to Make People Just*, 39–45.

5. Rawls, Chapter 3.

6. John C. Harsanyi, *Essays on Ethics, Social Behavior, and Scientific Explanation* (Dordrecht, Reidel, 1976).

7. See David Gauthier, "Justice and Natural Endowment," *Social Theory and Practice*, special issue (1974) and my article "Justice as Desert," in that same issue of *Social Theory and Practice*, and my *The Demands of Justice*. In this early work, I endorsed what I now call the compromise view over the maximin and utilitarian views. Unfortunately, at the time I identified its requirements with a basic-needs minimum, failing to see both that this minimum only becomes appropriate once distant peoples and future generations are taken into account, and that once they are taken into account the three views coincide in their practical requirements, or so I shall argue in this chapter.

8. See, for example, Norman Daniels, *Reading Rawls* (New York: Basic Books, 1975) and my *Justice: Alternative Political Perspectives*, 2d ed. (Belmont, CA: Wadsworth, 1991).

9. It has been estimated that the cost of the cereal in a typical three-dollar box of cereal is ten cents. (WBBM, "Report on the Economic Impact of the Flooding of the Mississippi" July 10, 1993.)

10. Bob Bergland, "Attacking the Problem of World Hunger," *The National Forum* 69, no. 2 (1979): 4.

11. Henry Shue, *Basic Rights* (Princeton: Princeton University Press, 1980), Chapter 7.

12. For a discussion of these causal connections, see Cheryl Silver, *One Earth One Future* (Washington, D.C., National Academy Press, 1990); Bill McKibben, *The End of Nature* (New York, Anchor Books, 1989); Jeremy Leggett, ed., *Global Warming* (New York, Oxford University Press, 1990); Lester Brown, ed., *The World Watch Reader* (New York, Norton, 1991).

13. Janet Besecker and Phil Elder, "Lifeboat Ethics: A Reply to Hardin," in *Readings in Ecology, Energy and Human Society: Contemporary Perspectives*, ed. William R. Burdi, Jr. (New York, Harper & Row, 1977), 229.

14. Currently, the United States which constitutes 6 percent of the world's population consumes 30 percent of the world's natural resources. There is no way that U.S. resource consumption can be matched by developing and underdeveloped countries, and even if it could, doing so would

clearly lead to ecological disaster. See Constance Mungall and Digby
McLaren, eds., *Planet under Stress.* (Oxford: Oxford University Press, 1990)
and Frances Lappe and Joseph Collins, *World Hunger: Twelve Myths* (New
York: Grove Press, 1986).
15. Ronald Dworkin, "The Original Position," *University of Chicago Law
Review* 40 (1973).
16. Rawls, 101.
17. Robert Nozick, *Anarchy, State and Utopia* (New York, Basic Books, 1974)
and Michael Sandel, *Liberalism and the Limits of Justice* (Cambridge,
Cambridge University Press, 1982).
18. Elizabeth Wolgast, *The Grammar of Justice* (Ithaca, NY: Cornell
University Press, 1987) and Thomas Moody, "Liberal Conceptions of the
Self and Autonomy" in *Freedom, Equality and Social Change*, ed. James P.
Sterba and Creighton Peden (Lewiston, Edwin Mellon Press, 1989).
19. Richard Miller, "Rawls and Marxism," *Philosophy and Public Affairs* 3
(1974).
20. This topic will be discussed in Chapter 8.

3

Libertarianism: The Ideal of Liberty

Ideals that are universally accepted are invariably ideals that are differently understood, and in this respect liberty is no exception. Thus, those who favor liberty but condemn license do not understand liberty in the same way as, for example, those who defend an absolute freedom of speech. The former understand liberty as being free to do what one ought; the latter understand liberty as being free to do what one wants. Nor, for that matter, do those who favor institutions of private property and a restriction of social services usually understand liberty in the same way as those who favor socialization of the means of production along with an expansion of social services. The former understand liberty to be constrained only by positive acts (that is, acts of commission) that prevent people from doing what they are otherwise able to do; the latter understand liberty to also be constrained by negative acts (that is, acts of omission) that prevent people from doing what they are otherwise able to do.

Libertarianism, however, is the only contemporary social and political view that consistently takes an ideal of liberty to be its core requirement. In recent elections Libertarian party candidates have not done very well. Nevertheless, Ronald Reagan, George Bush, and Margaret Thatcher, whose views on economic issues are close to libertarianism, were politically successful and did succeed in refashioning the economies of their respective nations. It is this ideal of liberty that will be the focus of discussion in this chapter.

Libertarians have defended their ideal in basically two ways.[1] Some libertarians, following Herbert Spencer, have (1) taken a right to liberty as basic and (2) derived all other rights from this right to liberty. Other libertarians, following John Locke, have (1) taken a set of rights, including typically a right to life and a right to property, as basic and

(2) defined liberty as the absence of constraints in the exercise of these rights. Now both groups of libertarians regard liberty as the ultimate social and political ideal, but they do so for different reasons. For Spencerian libertarians, liberty is the ultimate social and political ideal because all other rights are derived from a right to liberty. For Lockean libertarians, liberty is the ultimate social and political ideal because liberty just is the absence of constraints in the exercise of people's fundamental rights.

SPENCERIAN LIBERTARIANS

Let us begin by considering the view of those libertarians, like John Hospers, who take a right to liberty to be basic and define all other rights in terms of this right to liberty. According to this view, liberty is usually interpreted in this way.

> *The Want Interpretation of Liberty*: Liberty is being unconstrained by other persons from doing what one wants.

This interpretation limits the scope of liberty in two ways. First, not all constraints, whatever their source, count as a restriction of liberty; the constraints must come from other persons. People who are constrained by natural forces from getting to the top of Mount Everest do not lack liberty in this regard. Second, constraints that have their source in other persons, but that do not run counter to an individual's wants, constrain without restricting that individual's liberty. Thus, for people who do not want to hear Beethoven's Fifth Symphony, the fact that others have effectively proscribed its performance does not restrict their liberty, even though it does constrain what they are able to do.

Of course, libertarians may wish to argue that even such constraints can be seen to restrict a person's liberty once we take into account the fact that people normally want, or have a general desire, to be unconstrained by others. But other philosophers have thought that the possibility of such constraints points to a serious defect in this conception of liberty,[2] which can only be remedied by adopting the following broader interpretation of liberty.

> *The Ability Interpretation of Liberty*: Liberty is being unconstrained by other persons from doing what one is able to do.

Applying this interpretation to the previous example, we find that people's liberty to hear Beethoven's Fifth Symphony would be restricted even if they did not want to hear it (and even if, perchance, they did not want to be unconstrained by others) since other people would still be constraining them from doing what they are able to do.

Confident that problems of defining liberty can be overcome in some satisfactory manner, libertarians go on to characterize their social and political ideal as requiring that each person should have the greatest amount of liberty commensurate with the same liberty for all. From this ideal, libertarians claim that a number of more specific requirements, in particular a right to life; a right to freedom of speech, press, and assembly; and a right to property can be derived.

Here it is important to observe that the libertarian's right to life is not a right to receive from others the goods and resources necessary for preserving one's life. It is not a right to a social minimum: it is simply a right not to be killed unjustly. Correspondingly, the libertarian's right to property is not a right to receive from others the goods and resources necessary to secure a social minimum, but rather a right to acquire goods and resources either by initial acquisitions or by voluntary agreements.

Of course, libertarians would allow that it would be nice of the rich to share their surplus resources with the poor. Nevertheless, libertarians deny that government has a duty to provide for such needs. Some good things, such as the provision of welfare to the needy, are requirements of charity rather than justice, libertarians claim. Accordingly, failure to make such provisions is neither blameworthy nor punishable. According to libertarians, such acts of charity should not be coercively required. For this reason, libertarians are opposed to any coercively supported social minimum.

LOCKEAN LIBERTARIANS

The same opposition to a coercively supported social minimum characterizes those libertarians who take a set of rights, typically including a right to life and a right to property, as basic and then interpret liberty in this way.

The Rights Interpretation of Liberty: Liberty is being unconstrained by other persons from doing what one has a right to do.

According to this view, a right to life is simply a right not to be killed unjustly; it is not a right to receive a social minimum. Correspondingly, a right to property is a right to acquire property either by initial acquisitions or by voluntary transactions; it is not a right to receive from others whatever goods and resources one needs to maintain oneself. Understanding a right to life and a right to property in this way, libertarians reject any coercively supported social minimum as a violation of liberty.

A PARTIAL DEFENSE

In support of their view, libertarians have advanced the following examples. The first two are taken from Milton Friedman, the last from Robert Nozick.

In the first example, you are to suppose that you and three friends are walking along the street and you happen to notice and retrieve a $100 bill lying on the pavement. Suppose a rich fellow had been by earlier throwing away $100 bills, and you have been lucky enough to find one of them. Now according to Friedman, it would be nice of you to share your good fortune with your friends. Nevertheless, they have no right to demand that you do so, and hence, they would not be justified in forcing you to share the $100 bill with them. Similarly, Friedman would have us believe that it would be nice of us to provide a social minimum to the less fortunate members of our society. Nevertheless, the less fortunate members have no right to a social minimum, and hence, they would not be justified in forcing us to provide such.

The second example, which Friedman regards as analogous to the first, involves supposing that there are four Robinson Crusoes each marooned on four uninhabited islands in the same neighborhood. One of these Crusoes happens to land on a large and fruitful island which enables him to live easily and well. The others happen to land on tiny and rather barren islands from which they can barely scratch a living. Suppose one day they discover the existence of each other. Now according to Friedman, it would be nice of the fortunate Robinson Crusoe to share the resources of his island with the other three Crusoes, but the other three Crusoes have no right to demand that he share those resources, and it would be wrong for them to force him to do so. Correspondingly, Friedman thinks it would be nice of us to provide the less fortunate in our society with a social minimum, but the less fortunate have no right to demand that we do so, and it would be wrong for them to force us to provide such.

In the third example, Robert Nozick asks us to imagine that we are in a society that has just distributed income according to some ideal pattern, possibly a pattern of equality. We are to further imagine that in such a society someone with the talents of Michael Jordan offers to play basketball for us provided that he receives, let us say, one dollar from every home game ticket that is sold. Suppose we agree to these terms and two million people attend the home games to see this new Michael Jordan play, thereby securing for him an income of two million dollars. Since such an income would surely upset the initial pattern of income distribution whatever that happened to be, Nozick contends that this illustrates how an ideal of liberty upsets the

patterns required by other social and political ideals, and hence, calls
for their rejection.

SPENCERIAN LIBERTARIANS AND THE PROBLEM OF CONFLICT

To evaluate the libertarian view, let us begin with the ideal of liberty
as defended by Spencerian libertarians and consider a typical conflict
situation between the rich and the poor. In this situation, the rich have
more than enough resources to satisfy their basic needs. By contrast,
the poor lack the resources to meet their most basic needs even though
they have tried all the means available to them that Spencerian libertarians regard as legitimate for acquiring such resources. Under
circumstances like these, libertarians usually maintain that the rich
should have the liberty not to be interfered with in using their
resources to satisfy their luxury needs if they so wish. Spencerian libertarians recognize that this liberty might well be enjoyed at the
expense of the satisfaction of the most basic needs of the poor; they
just think that liberty always has priority over other social and political ideals. Since they assume that the liberty of the poor is not at stake
in such conflict situations, it is easy for them to conclude that the rich
should not be required to sacrifice their liberty so that the basic needs
of the poor may be met.

Of course, Spencerian libertarians allow that it would be nice of the
rich to share their surplus resources with the poor, just as Milton
Friedman would allow that it would be nice of you to share a found
$100 with your friends, and nice of the rich-islanded Robinson Crusoe
to share his resources with the poor-islanded Robinson Crusoes.
Nevertheless, according to Spencerian libertarians, such acts of charity cannot be required because the liberty of the poor is not thought to
be at stake in such conflict situations.

In fact, however, the liberty of the poor is at stake in such conflict situations. What is at stake is the liberty of the poor not to be interfered
with in taking from the surplus possessions of the rich what is necessary to satisfy their basic needs.[3]

Needless to say, Spencerian libertarians would want to deny that
the poor have this liberty. But how could they justify such a denial?
As this liberty of the poor has been specified, it is not a positive right
to receive something, but a negative right of noninterference. Nor
will it do for Spencerian libertarians to appeal to a right to life or a
right to property to rule out such a liberty because, on the Spencerian
view, liberty is basic and all other rights are derived from a right to
liberty. Clearly, what Spencerian libertarians must do is recognize
the existence of such a liberty, and then claim that it conflicts with
other liberties of the rich. But when Spencerian libertarians see that

this is the case, they are often genuinely surprised, one might even say rudely awakened, for they had not previously seen the conflict between the rich and the poor as a conflict of liberties.[4]

When the conflict between the rich and the poor is viewed as a conflict of liberties, we can either say that the rich should have the liberty not to be interfered with in using their surplus resources for luxury purposes, or we can say that the poor should have the liberty not to be interfered with in taking from the rich what they require to meet their basic needs. If we choose one liberty, we must reject the other. What needs to be determined, therefore, is which liberty is morally preferable: the liberty of the rich or the liberty of the poor.

Two Principles

In order to see that the liberty of the poor not to be interfered with in taking from the surplus resources of the rich what is required to meet their basic needs is morally preferable to the liberty of the rich not to be interfered with in using their surplus resources for luxury purposes, we need to appeal to one of the most fundamental principles of morality, one that is common to all political perspectives. This is the "Ought" Implies "Can" Principle.

> People are not morally required to do what they lack the power to do or what would involve so great a sacrifice that it would be unreasonable to ask them to perform such an action, and/or in the case of severe conflicts of interest, unreasonable to require them to perform such an action.[5]

Suppose I promised to attend a departmental meeting on Friday, but on Thursday I am involved in a serious car accident that leaves me in a coma. Surely, it is no longer the case that I ought to attend the meeting now that I lack the power to do so. Or suppose instead that on Thursday I develop a severe case of pneumonia for which I am hospitalized. Surely, I could legitimately claim that I cannot attend the meeting on the grounds that the risk to my health involved in attending is a sacrifice that it would be unreasonable to ask me to bear. Or suppose the risk to my health from having pneumonia is not so serious that it would be unreasonable to ask me to attend the meeting (a supererogatory request); it might still be serious enough to be unreasonable to require my attendance at the meeting (a demand that is backed up by blame or coercion).

What is distinctive about this formulation of the "ought" implies "can" principle is that it claims that the requirements of morality cannot, all things considered, be unreasonable to ask, and/or in cases of severe conflict of interest, unreasonable to require people to abide by. The principle claims that reason and morality must be linked in an appropriate way, especially if we are going to be able justifiably to use blame or coercion to get people to abide by the requirements of morality. It should be noted, however, that although major figures in the history of philosophy, and most philosophers today, including virtually all libertarian philosophers, accept this linkage between reason and morality, this linkage is not usually conceived to be part of the "ought" implies "can" principle. Nevertheless, I claim that there are good reasons for associating this linkage with the principle, namely, our use of the word *can* as in the example just given, and the natural progression from logical, physical, and psychological possibility found in the traditional "ought" implies "can" principle to the notion of moral possibility found in this formulation of the principle. In any case, the acceptability of this formulation of the "ought" implies "can" principle is determined by the virtually universal acceptance of its components and not by the manner in which I have proposed to join those components together.

Now applying the "ought" implies "can" principle to the case at hand, it seems clear that the poor have it within their power willingly to relinquish such an important liberty as the liberty not to be interfered with in taking from the rich what they require to meet their basic needs. Nevertheless, it would be unreasonable to ask or require them to make so great a sacrifice. In the extreme case, it would involve asking or requiring the poor to sit back and starve to death. Of course, the poor may have no real alternative to relinquishing this liberty. To do anything else may involve worse consequences for themselves and their loved ones and may invite a painful death. Accordingly, we may expect that the poor would acquiesce, albeit unwillingly, to a political system that denies them the right to welfare supported by such a liberty, at the same time that we recognize that such a system imposes an unreasonable sacrifice upon the poor—a sacrifice that we can not morally blame the poor for trying to evade.[6] Analogously, we might expect that a woman whose life was threatened would submit to a rapist's demands, at the same time that we recognize the utter unreasonableness of those demands.

By contrast, it would not be unreasonable to ask and require the rich to sacrifice the liberty to meet some of their luxury needs so that the poor can have the liberty to meet their basic needs.[7] Naturally, we might expect that the rich, for reasons of self-interest and past contribution, might be disinclined to make such a sacrifice. We might even suppose that the past contribution of the rich provides a good reason for not sacrificing their liberty to use their surplus for luxury purposes. Yet, unlike the poor, the rich could not claim that relinquishing such a liberty would involve so great a sacrifice that it would be unreasonable to ask and require them to make it; unlike the poor, the rich could be morally blameworthy for failing to make such a sacrifice.

Notice that by virtue of the "ought" implies "can" principle, this argument establishes that:

1a. Since it would be unreasonable to ask or require the poor to sacrifice the liberty not to be interfered with when taking from the surplus resources of the rich what is necessary to meet their basic needs,

1b. it is not the case that the poor are morally required to make such a sacrifice.

2a. Since it would not be unreasonable to ask and require the rich to sacrifice the liberty not to be interfered with when using their surplus resources for luxury purposes,

2b. it may be the case that the rich are morally required to make such a sacrifice.

What the argument does not establish is that it is the case that the rich are *morally required* to sacrifice (some of) their surplus so that the basic needs of the poor can be met. To clearly establish that conclusion, we need to appeal to a principle, which is, in fact, simply the contrapositive of the "ought" implies "can" principle.[8] It is the Conflict Resolution Principle.

> What people are morally required to do is what is either reasonable to ask everyone affected to accept, or in the case of severe conflicts of interest, reasonable to require everyone affected to accept.

While the "ought" implies "can" principle claims that if any action is *not reasonable to ask or require* a person to do, all things considered, that action is *not morally required* for that person, all things considered, the conflict resolution principle claims that if any action is *morally required* for a person to do, all things considered, that action is *reasonable to ask or require* that person to do, all things considered.

Now applying the conflict resolution principle to our example of severe conflict between the rich and the poor, there are three possible moral resolutions.

I. A moral resolution that would require the rich to sacrifice the liberty not to be interfered with when using their surplus resources for luxury purposes so that the poor can have the liberty not to be interfered with when taking from the surplus resources of the rich what is necessary to meet their basic needs.

II. A moral resolution that would require the poor to sacrifice the liberty not to be interfered with when taking from the surplus resources of the rich what is necessary to meet their basic needs so that the rich can have the liberty not to be interfered with when using their surplus resources for luxury purposes.

III. A moral resolution that would require the rich and the poor to accept the results of a power struggle in which both the rich and the poor are at liberty to appropriate and use the surplus resources of the rich.

Applying our previous discussion of the "ought" implies "can" principle to these three possible moral resolutions, it is clear that 1a (it would be unreasonable to ask or require the poor . . .) rules out II, but 2a (it would not be unreasonable to ask and require the rich . . .) does not rule out I. But what about III? Some libertarians have contended that III is the proper resolution of severe conflicts of interest between the rich and the poor.[9] But a resolution, like III, that sanctions the results of a power struggle between the rich and the poor, is a resolution that, by and large, favors the rich over the poor. So all things considered, it would be no more reasonable to require the poor to accept III than it would be to require them to accept II. This means that only I satisfies the conflict resolution principle by being a resolution that is reasonable to require everyone affected to accept. Consequently, if we assume that however else we specify the requirements of morality, they cannot violate the "ought" implies "can" principle or the conflict resolution principle, it follows that, despite what Spencerian libertarians claim, the basic right to liberty endorsed by them, as determined by a weighing of the relevant competing liberties according to these two principles, actually favors the liberty of the poor over the liberty of the rich.

Yet couldn't Spencerian libertarians object to this conclusion, claiming that it would be unreasonable to require the rich to sacrifice the liberty to meet some of their luxury needs so that the poor could have the liberty to meet their basic needs? As has been pointed out, libertarians don't usually see the situation as a conflict of liberties, but suppose they did. How plausible would such an objection be? Not very plausible at all.

Consider: What are Spencerian libertarians going to say about the poor? Isn't it clearly unreasonable to require the poor to sacrifice the liberty to meet their basic needs so that the rich can have the liberty to meet their luxury needs? Isn't it clearly unreasonable to require the poor to sit back and starve to death? If it is, then, there is no resolution of this conflict that would be reasonable to require both the rich and the poor to accept. But that would mean that libertarians could not be putting forth a moral resolution because according to the conflict resolution principle, in cases of severe conflict of interest, a moral res-olution resolves conflicts of interest in ways that it would be reasonable to require everyone affected to accept. Therefore, as long as libertarians think of themselves as putting forth a moral resolution for cases of severe conflict of interest, they cannot allow that it would be unreasonable *both* to require the rich to sacrifice the liberty to meet some of their luxury needs in order to benefit the poor and to require the poor to sacrifice the liberty to meet their basic needs in order to benefit the rich. But I submit that if one of these requirements is to be judged reasonable, then, by any neutral assessment, it must be the requirement that the rich sacrifice the liberty to meet some of their lux-ury needs so that the poor can have the liberty to meet their basic needs. There is no other plausible resolution, if libertarians intend to put forth a moral resolution.

But might not Spencerian libertarians hold that putting forth a moral resolution requires nothing more than being willing to univer-salize one's fundamental commitments? Surely, we have no difficulty imagining the rich being willing to universalize their commitments to relatively strong property rights. At the same time, we have no diffi-culty imagining the poor and their advocates being willing to universalize their commitment to relatively weak property rights. However, if a libertarian moral resolution is interpreted in this fash-ion, it would not be able to provide a basis for resolving conflicts of interest between the rich and the poor in a reasonable fashion. And without such a basis for conflict resolution, how could we flourish, as libertarians claim we would, under a minimal state?[10] For societies to flourish in this fashion, the libertarian ideal must resolve severe con-flicts of interest in ways that it would be reasonable to require everyone affected to accept. But as we have seen, that requirement can be satisfied only if the rich sacrifice the liberty to meet their luxury needs so that the poor can have the liberty to meet their basic needs.

It should also be noted that this case for restricting the liberty of the rich depends upon the willingness of the poor to take advantage of whatever opportunities are available to them to engage in mutually beneficial work, so that failure of the poor to take advantage of such opportunities would normally cancel or at least significantly reduce the obligation of the rich to restrict their own liberty for the benefit of the poor.[11] In addition, the poor would be required to return the equivalent of any surplus possessions they have taken from the rich once they are able to do so and still satisfy their basic needs. Nor would the poor be required to keep the liberty to which they are enti-tled. They could give up part of it, or all of it, or risk losing it on the chance of gaining a greater share of liberties or other social goods.[12]

Consequently, the case for restricting the liberty of the rich for the benefit of the poor is neither unconditional nor inalienable.

Of course, there will be cases where the poor fail to satisfy their basic needs, not because of any direct restriction of liberty on the part of the rich but because the poor are in such dire need that they are unable even to attempt to take from the rich what they require to meet their basic needs. In such cases, the rich would not be performing any act of commission that prevents the poor from taking what they require. Yet, even in such cases, the rich would normally be performing acts of commission that prevent other persons from aiding the poor by taking from the rich's own surplus possessions. And when assessed from a moral point of view, restricting the liberty of these other persons would not be morally justified for the very same reason that restricting the liberty of the poor to meet their own basic needs would not be morally justified: It would not be reasonable to require all of those affected to accept such a restriction of liberty.

The Benefit of the Poor

Nevertheless, Spencerian libertarians might respond that even assuming a right to welfare could be morally justified on the basis of the liberty of the poor not to be interfered with when taking from the rich in order to meet their basic needs and the liberty of third parties not to be interfered with when taking from the rich to provide for the basic needs of the poor, the poor still would be better off without the enforcement of such a right.[13] For example, it might be argued that when people are not forced through taxation to support a right to welfare, they are both more productive, since they are able to keep more of what they produce, and more charitable, since they tend to give more freely to those in need when they are not forced to do so. As a result, so the argument goes, the poor would benefit more from the increased charity of a libertarian society than they would from the guaranteed minimum of a welfare state.

Yet, surely it is difficult to comprehend how the poor could be better off in a libertarian society, assuming, as seems likely, that they would experience a considerable loss of self-respect once they had to depend upon the uncertainties of charity for the satisfaction of their basic needs without the protection of a guaranteed minimum. It is also difficult to comprehend how people who are presently so opposed to a guaranteed minimum would turn out to be so charitable to the poor in a libertarian society.

Moreover, in a libertarian society, providing for the needs of the poor would involve an impossible coordination problem. For if the duty to help the poor is at best supererogatory, as libertarians claim, then no one can legitimately force anyone who does not consent to provide help. The will of the majority on this issue could not legitimately be imposed upon dissenters.[14] Assuming then that providing for the needs of the poor requires coordinated action on a broad front, such coordination could not be achieved in a libertarian society because it would first require a near-unanimous agreement of all its members.[15]

Nevertheless, it might still be argued that the greater productivity of the more talented people in a libertarian society would provide increased employment opportunities and increased voluntary welfare assistance which would benefit the poor more than a guaranteed minimum would in a welfare state. But this simply could not occur. For if the more talented members of a society provided sufficient employment opportunities and voluntary welfare assistance to enable the poor to meet their basic needs, then the conditions for invoking a right to a guaranteed minimum in a welfare state would not arise, since the poor are first required to take advantage of whatever employment opportunities and voluntary welfare assistance are available to them before they can legitimately invoke such a right.[16] Consequently, when *sufficient* employment opportunities and voluntary welfare assistance obtain, there would be no practical difference in this regard between a libertarian society and a welfare state, since neither would justify invoking a right to a guaranteed minimum. Only when *insufficient* employment opportunities and voluntary welfare assistance obtain would there be a practical difference between a libertarian society and a welfare state, and then it would clearly benefit the poor to be able to invoke the right to a guaranteed minimum in a welfare state. Consequently, given the conditional nature of the right to welfare, and the practical possibility, and in most cases, the actuality of insufficient employment opportunities and voluntary welfare assistance obtaining, there is no reason to think that the poor would be better off without the enforcement of such a right.[17]

In brief, if a right to liberty is taken to be basic, then, contrary to what Spencerian libertarians claim, not only would a right to welfare be morally required but also such a right would clearly benefit the poor.

LOCKEAN LIBERTARIANS AND THE PROBLEM OF CONFLICT

Let us now consider whether these same conclusions can be established against Lockean libertarians who take a set of rights, typically including a right to life and a right to property, as basic and then interpret liberty as being unconstrained by other persons from doing what one has a right to do. According to this view, a right to life is understood as a right not to be killed unjustly, and a right to property is understood as a right to acquire goods and resources either by initial acquisition or by voluntary agreement. In order to evaluate this view, we must determine what is entailed by these rights.

Presumably, a right to life understood as a right not to be killed unjustly would not be violated by defensive measures designed to protect one's person from life-threatening attacks.[18] Yet, would this right be violated when the rich prevent the poor from taking what they require to satisfy their basic needs? Obviously, as a consequence of such preventive actions poor people sometimes do starve to death. Have the rich, then, in contributing to this result, killed the poor, or simply have they let them die; and, if they have killed the poor, have they done so unjustly?

Sometimes the rich, in preventing the poor from taking what they require to meet their basic needs, would not in fact be killing the poor, but only causing them to be physically or mentally debilitated. Yet since such preventive acts involve resisting the life-preserving activities of the poor, when the poor do die as a consequence of such acts, it seems clear that the rich would be killing the poor, whether intentionally or unintentionally.

Libertarians would want to argue that such killing is simply a consequence of the legitimate exercise of property rights, and hence, not unjust. But to understand why libertarians are mistaken in this regard, let us appeal again to those fundamental principles of morality, the "ought" implies "can" principle and the conflict resolution principle. In this context, these principles can be used to assess two opposing accounts of property rights. According to the first account, a right to property is not conditional upon whether other persons have sufficient opportunities and resources to satisfy their basic needs. This view holds that the initial acquisition and voluntary agreement of some can leave others, through no fault of their own, dependent upon charity for the satisfaction of their most basic needs. By contrast, according to the second account, initial acquisition and voluntary agreement can confer title of property on all goods and resources except those surplus goods and resources of the rich that are required to satisfy the basic needs of those poor who through no fault of their own lack opportunities and resources to satisfy their own basic needs.

Recall that with respect to the Spencerian view, there were two interpretations of the basic right to liberty on which the view is grounded: one interpretation ignores the liberty of the poor not be interfered with when taking from the surplus possessions of the rich what they require to meet their basic needs; the other gives that liberty priority over the liberty of the rich not be interfered with when using their surplus for luxury purposes. Here too there are two interpretations of the right to property on which the Lockean view is grounded: one interpretation regards the right to property as *not* conditional upon the resources and opportunities available to others; the other regards the right to property as conditional upon the resources and opportunities available to others. And just as in the case of the Spencerian view, here we need to appeal to those fundamental principles of morality, the "ought" implies "can" principle and the conflict resolution principle, to decide which interpretation is morally acceptable.

It is clear that only the unconditional interpretation of property rights would generally justify the killing of the poor as a legitimate exercise of the property rights of the rich. Yet, it would be unreasonable to require the poor to accept anything other than some version of the conditional interpretation of property rights. Moreover, according to the conditional interpretation, it does not matter whether the poor would actually die or are only physically or mentally debilitated as a result of such acts of prevention. Either result would preclude property rights from arising. Of course, the poor may have no real alternative to acquiescing to a political system modeled after the unconditional interpretation of property rights, even though such a system imposes an unreasonable sacrifice upon them—a sacrifice that we could not blame them for trying to evade. At the same time, although the rich may be disinclined to do so, it would not be unreasonable to require them to accept a political system modeled after the conditional interpretation of property rights—the interpretation favored by the poor.

Consequently, if we assume that however else we specify the requirements of morality, they cannot violate the "ought" implies "can" principle and the conflict resolution principle, it follows that, despite what Lockean libertarians claim, the right to life and the right to property endorsed by them actually support a right to welfare.

Now it might be objected that the rights that this argument establishes from libertarian premises are not the same as the rights to welfare endorsed by welfare liberals and socialists. This is correct. We could mark this difference by referring to the rights that this argument establishes as "negative welfare rights" and by referring to the rights endorsed by welfare liberals and socialists as "positive welfare rights." The significance of this difference is that a person's negative welfare rights can be violated only when other people through acts of commission interfere with their exercise, whereas a person's positive welfare rights can be violated not only by such acts of commission but by acts of omission as well. Nonetheless, this difference will have little practical import. For once libertarians come to recognize the legitimacy of negative welfare rights, then in order not to be subject to the discretion of rightholders in choosing when and how to exercise these rights, libertarians will tend to favor the only morally legitimate way of preventing the exercise of such rights: they will institute adequate positive welfare rights that will then take precedence over the exercise of negative welfare rights. Accordingly, if libertarians adopt this morally legitimate way of preventing the exercise of such rights, they will end up endorsing the same sort of welfare institutions favored by welfare liberals and socialists.

In brief, I have argued that a libertarian ideal of liberty can be seen to support a guaranteed social minimum through an application of the "ought" implies "can" principle and the conflict resolution principle to severe conflicts between the rich and the poor. In one interpretation, these principles support such a minimum by favoring the liberty of the poor over the liberty of the rich. In another interpretation, the principle supports such rights by favoring a conditional right to property over an unconditional right to property. In either interpretation, what is crucial to the derivation of this guaranteed social minimum is the claim that it would be unreasonable to require the poor to deny their basic needs and accept anything less than a guaranteed social minimum as the condition for their willing cooperation.

LIBERTARIAN OBJECTIONS

In his book, *Individuals and Their Rights*, Tibor Machan criticizes the preceding argument that a libertarian ideal of liberty leads to a right to welfare, accepting its theoretical thrust but denying its practical significance.[19] He appreciates the force of the argument enough to grant that if the type of conflict cases that we have described between the rich and the poor actually obtained, the poor would have a right to welfare. But he denies that such cases—in which the poor have done all that they legitimately can to satisfy their basic needs in a libertarian society—actually obtain. "Normally," he writes, "persons do not lack the opportunities and resources to satisfy their basic needs."[20]

But this response virtually concedes everything that the preceding argument intended to establish. For the poor's right to welfare is not claimed to be unconditional. Rather it is said to be conditional principally upon the poor doing all that they legitimately can to meet their own basic needs. So it follows that only when the poor lack sufficient opportunity to satisfy their own basic needs would their right to welfare have any practical moral force. Accordingly, on libertarian grounds, Machan has conceded the legitimacy of just the kind of right to welfare that the argument hoped to establish.

The only difference that remains is a practical one. Machan thinks that virtually all of the poor have sufficient opportunities and

resources to satisfy their basic needs and that, therefore, a right to welfare has no practical moral force. In contrast, I would think that many
of the poor do not have sufficient opportunities and resources to satisfy their basic needs and that, therefore, a right to welfare has
considerable practical moral force.

But isn't this practical disagreement resolvable? For who could deny
that most of the 1.2 billion people who are currently living in conditions of absolute poverty "lack the opportunities and resources to
satisfy their basic needs?"[21] And even within our own country, it is
estimated that some 32 million Americans live below the official
poverty index, and that one-fifth of American children are growing up
in poverty.[22] Surely, it is impossible to deny that many of these
Americans also "lack the opportunities and resources to satisfy their
basic needs." Given the impossibility of reasonably denying these fac-
tual claims, Machan would have to concede that the right to welfare,
which he grants can be theoretically established on libertarian
premises, also has practical moral force.[23]

Douglas Rasmussen has developed another libertarian challenge to
the previous argument that begins by conceding what Machan
denied—that the poor can lack the opportunity to satisfy their basic
needs.[24] Rasmussen distinguishes two ways that this can occur. In one
case, only a few of the poor lack the opportunity to satisfy their basic
needs. Here, Rasmussen contends that libertarian property rights still
apply even though the poor that are in need ought to take from the surplus property of the rich what they need for survival. Since libertarian
property rights still apply, Rasmussen contends that the poor who do
take from the legal property of the rich can be arrested and tried for
their actions, but what their punishment should be, Rasmussen contends, should simply be left up to judges to decide.[25] Rasmussen also
rejects the suggestion that the law should make an exception for the
poor in such cases on the grounds that one can never have perfect symmetry between what is moral and what the law requires.[26]

But why should the question of punishment be simply left up to the
judges to decide? If the judicial proceedings determine what is
assumed in this case—that the poor morally ought to take from the
legal property of the rich what they need for survival, then it is difficult to see on what grounds a judge could inflict punishment. Surely,
if it would be unreasonable to require the poor to do anything contrary to meeting their basic needs at minimal cost to the rich, it would
be equally unreasonable to punish the poor for actually doing just
that—meeting their basic needs at minimal cost to the rich.

Nor will it do to claim that we cannot expect symmetry between
what morality requires and what the law requires in this case. Of
course, there is no denying that sometimes the law can justifiably

require us to do what is morally wrong. In such cases, opposing the law, even when what it requires is immoral, would do more harm than good. This can occur when there is a bona fide disagreement over whether what the law requires is morally wrong (for example, the *Roe v. Wade* decision), with those in favor of the law justifiably thinking that it is morally right and those against the law justifiably thinking that it is morally wrong. When this occurs, failing to obey the law, even when what it requires is immoral, could, by undermining the legal system, do more harm than good. However, in our case of severe conflict of interest between the rich and the poor, nothing of the sort obtains. In our case, it is judged that the poor ought to take from the legal property of the rich and that no other moral imperative favoring the rich overrides this moral imperative favoring the poor. So it is clear in this case that there are no grounds for upholding any asymmetry between what morality and the law require. Accordingly, the law in this case should be changed to favor the poor.

However, Rasmussen distinguishes another case in which the poor lack the opportunity to satisfy their basic needs.[27] In this case, so many of the poor lack the opportunity to satisfy their basic needs that Rasmussen claims that libertarian property rights no longer apply. Here, Rasmussen contends that morality requires that the poor should take what they need for survival from the legal property of the rich and that the rich should not refuse assistance. Still Rasmussen contends that the poor have no right to assistance in this case, nor the rich presumably any corresponding obligation to help the poor because "the situation cannot be judged in social and political terms."[28]

But why cannot the situation be judged in social and political terms? If we know what the moral directives of the rich and the poor are in this case, as Rasmussen admits that we do, why would we not be justified in setting up a legal system or altering an existing legal system so that the poor would have a guaranteed right to welfare? Now it may be that Rasmussen is imagining a situation where it is not possible for the basic needs of everyone to be met. Such situations are truly lifeboat cases. But while such cases are difficult to resolve (maybe only a chance mechanism would offer a reasonable resolution) they surely do not represent the typical conflict situation between the rich and the poor. For in such situations, it is recognized that it is possible to meet everyone's basic needs, and what is at issue is whether (some of) the nonbasic or luxury needs of the rich should be sacrificed so that everyone's basic needs can be met. So when dealing with typical conflict situations between the rich and the poor there is no justification for not securing a legal system that reflects the moral directives in these cases.

In sum, both Machan's and Rasmussen's objections to grounding a right to welfare on libertarian premises have been answered.

Machan's attempt to grant the theoretical validity of a libertarian right to welfare, but then deny its practical validity, fails once we recognize that there are many poor who lack the opportunities to satisfy their basic needs. Rasmussen's attempt to grant that there are poor who lack the opportunity to meet their basic needs, but then deny that the poor have any right to welfare, fails once we recognize that the moral directives that Rasmussen grants apply to the rich and the poor in severe conflict of interest cases provide ample justification for a right to welfare.

LEGITIMATE AUTHORITIES AND THE IDEAL OF LIBERTY

As we noted before, the basic problem with providing a justification for coercive institutions as legitimate authorities is that different social and political ideals might require different coercive institutions with different types of authorities for realizing those ideals. So if there were no way to show that one of these ideals is morally preferable, then there would be no way to show which coercive institutions and authorities are legitimate. In particular, if welfare liberalism and libertarianism require radically different coercive institutions, how would we know what institutions we should have? Fortunately, we need not face this problem with respect to welfare liberalism and libertarianism now that it has been shown that these two ideals agree in their practical requirements. Specifically, we have shown that the right to a social minimum endorsed by welfare liberals is also required by the libertarian's own ideal of liberty. Given then that welfare liberals and libertarians endorse the same guaranteed social minimum they can also agree on the type of coercive institutions that are needed to secure that social minimum.

What remains to be seen, however, is whether the practical reconciliation that we have found between the welfare liberal and libertarian ideals can be extended to other social and political ideals. If it can be extended, it seems clear that we will be able to justify coercive institutions that support a basic-needs minimum. But if we cannot achieve a practical reconciliation with these other ideals, the major problem with providing a justification for coercive institutions will remain unresolved.

Notes

1. Quite a few years ago Jeffrey Paul suggested to me this way of approaching libertarianism. More recently, Tibor Machan has recommended a more multifaceted approach that classifies libertarians as Austrian economic, contractarian, evolutionary, Lockean, Stirnerite, or objectivist. But as far as I can tell, all of the morally relevant issues are captured by the way I have interpreted Paul's approach.

2. Isaiah Berlin, *Four Essays on Liberty* (New York, Oxford University Press, 1969), 38–40.

3. It is not being assumed here that the surplus possessions of the rich are either justifiably or unjustifiably possessed by the rich. Moreover, according to Spencerian libertarians, it is an assessment of the liberties involved that determines whether the possession is justifiable or not.

4. See John Hospers, *Libertarianism* (Los Angeles, Nash, 1971), Chapter 7 and Tibor Machan, *Human Rights and Human Liberties* (Chicago, Nelson-Hall, 1975), 231–32.

5. I first appealed to this interpretation of the "ought" implies "can" principle to bring libertarians around to the practical requirements of welfare liberalism in an expanded version of an article entitled "Neo-Libertarianism," which appeared in the fall of 1979. In 1982, T. M. Scanlon in "Contractualism and Utilitarianism" *Utilitarianism and Beyond*, ed. by Amartya Sen and Bernard Williams (Cambridge: Cambridge University Press, 1982) appealed to much the same standard to arbitrate the debate between contractarians and utilitarians. In my judgment, however, this standard embedded in the "ought" implies "can" principle can be more effectively used in the debate with libertarians than in the debate with utilitarians, because sacrifices libertarians standardly seek to impose on the less advantaged are more outrageous and, hence, more easily shown to be contrary to reason.

6. See Chapter 8.

7. By the liberty of the rich to meet their luxury needs I continue to mean the liberty of the rich not to be interfered with when using their surplus possessions for luxury purposes. Similarly, by the liberty of the poor to meet their basic needs I continue to mean the liberty of the poor not to be interfered with when taking what they require to meet their basic needs from the surplus possessions of the rich.

8. The contrapositive of a proposition is logically implied by the original proposition. The contrapositive of "All **S** is **P**" is "All non-**P** is non-**S**" and vice versa.

9. See, for example, Eric Mack, "Individualism, Rights and the Open Society," in *The Libertarian Alternative*, ed. by Tibor Machan (Chicago, Nelson-Hall, 1974).

10. As further evidence, notice that those libertarians who justify a minimal state do so on grounds that such a state would arise from reasonable disagreements concerning the application of libertarian rights. They do not justify the minimal state on the grounds that it would be needed to keep in submission large numbers of people who could not come to see the reasonableness of those rights.

11. The employment opportunities offered to the poor must be honorable and supportive of self-respect. To do otherwise would be to offer the poor the opportunity to meet some of their basic needs at the cost of denying some of their other basic needs.

12. The poor cannot, however, give up the liberty to which their children are entitled.

13. John Hospers, "The Libertarian Manifesto," in *Morality in Practice*, 4th ed., ed. James P. Sterba (Belmont, CA: Wadsworth, 1993).

14. Sometimes advocates of libertarianism inconsistently contend that the duty to help others is supererogatory, but that a majority of a society could justifiably enforce such a duty on everyone. See Theodore Benditt, "The Demands of Justice," in *Economic Justice*, ed. Diana Meyers and Kenneth Kipnis (Totowa, NJ: Rowman & Allanheld, 1985), 108–120.

15. Sometimes advocates of libertarianism focus on the coordination problems that arise in welfare and socialist states concerning the provision of welfare and ignore the far more serious coordination problems that would arise in a night-watchman state. See Burton Leiser, "Vagrancy, Loitering and Economic Justice," in *Economic Justice*, ed. Meyers and Kipnis, 149–160.

16. This assumes, of course, that the talented members of a society have acquired whatever surplus they have by means that are morally legitimate according to the libertarian view.

17. It is true, of course, that if the rich could retain the resources that are used in a welfare state for meeting the basic needs of the poor, they might have the option of using those resources to increase employment opportunities beyond what obtains in any given welfare state, but this particular way of increasing employment opportunities would be counterproductive with respect to meeting basic needs overall, and particularly counterproductive with respect to meeting the basic needs of those who cannot work.

18. James P. Sterba, "Moral Approaches to Nuclear Strategy: A Critical Evaluation," *Canadian Journal of Philosophy* 12, special issue (1986): 75–109.

19. Tibor Machan, *Individuals and Their Rights* (La Salle, IL: Open Court, 1989), 100–111.

20. *Ibid.*, 107.

21. Alan Durning, "Life on the Brink," *World Watch* 3, no. 2 (1990): 24.

22. *Ibid.*, 29.

23. In correspondence, Machan has distinguished between poverty and hunger that results from natural causes and poverty and hunger that results from "political tyrannies" or from other human causes. Machan suggests that only the first sort of poverty and hunger need concern libertarians. But unless the victims are morally responsible for their fate, then, it seems to me, others will have at least a prima facie obligation not to interfere with relief efforts, even when those relief efforts happen to be utilizing their own surplus possessions.

24. Douglas Rasmussen, "Individual Rights and Human Flourishing," *Public Affairs Quarterly* (1989): 89–103.

25. *Ibid.*, 98.

26. *Ibid.*, 99.

27. *Ibid.*, 100.

28. *Ibid.*, 101.

4

Socialism: The Ideal of Equality

The ideal of equality is commonly associated with socialism. While libertarians endorse equality before the law and welfare liberals endorse equal opportunity, only socialists endorse a substantial ideal of equality as their core requirement. In the United States, a few socialists have been elected to office, but there has never been a viable socialist presidential candidate.[1] Yet, elsewhere there have been many successful socialist candidates. For example, the late Olof Palme led the Social Democrats back to power in Sweden and François Mitterrand was elected president of France. It is this ideal of equality that will be the focus of this chapter.

A CHARACTERIZATION OF THE IDEAL

For contemporary socialists, equality is the ultimate social and political ideal. More precisely, as Karl Marx expressed the ideal over a century ago, distribution is to proceed according to the principle from each according to his or her ability to each according to his or her needs.[2] So, the ideal is one of equality of need-fulfillment or self-realization.

Certainly at first hearing, this ideal might sound simply crazy to someone brought up in a capitalist society. The obvious objection to this ideal is, How can you get persons to contribute according to their ability if you are going to distribute income on the basis of people's needs and not on the basis of their contributions?

The answer, according to socialists, is to make the work that must be done in a society as much as possible enjoyable in itself. As a result, people will want to do the work they are capable of doing because they will find it intrinsically rewarding. To start, socialists might try to get people to accept presently existing, intrinsically rewarding jobs at lower salaries. For example, socialists might try to get top executives to work for $400,000 rather than $800,000 per year. Yet ultimately, socialists hope to make all jobs as intrinsically rewarding as possible so that after people are no longer working primarily for external rewards, when making their best contributions to society, distribution can proceed on the basis of need.

Socialists propose to implement their ideal, in part, by giving workers democratic control over the workplace.[3] The key idea here is that if workers have more to say about how they do their work, the work itself will be more intrinsically rewarding. As a consequence, they will be more motivated to work since the work itself will be meeting their needs.

Under democratic control, workers would vote directly on major issues, including principal management strategies and major policy changes, and indirectly through their representatives on the day-to-day business of management. In this way, the hierarchical structure that presently characterizes capitalist firms with its sharp distinction between workers and managers would be radically transformed as workers gain increasingly more control over the workplace. Socialists, of course, do not deny that civil disobedience or even revolutionary action may be needed to overcome opposition to extending democracy to the workplace.

Yet, even with democratic control of the workplace, there will be some jobs that probably can't be made intrinsically rewarding (for example, garbage collecting or changing bedpans). Socialists propose to divide such jobs in some equitable manner.[4] Some people might, for example, collect garbage one day per week and then work at intrinsically rewarding jobs the rest of the workweek. Others would change bedpans or do some other slop job one day per week, and then work at intrinsically rewarding jobs the other days of the workweek.

So socialists would want to make jobs as intrinsically rewarding as possible, in part, through democratic control of the workplace and an equitable assignment of unrewarding tasks. But how would socialists deal with people who not only want an intrinsically rewarding job but also want the rewards that come from a good income? Without providing income differentials, how would socialists motivate such people to contribute according to their ability?

Surely, socialists would grant that some income differentials would be necessary to motivate people to make their best contributions. But socialists would strive to keep such differentials to a minimum by making the more talented members of society keenly aware of the social costs of having greater income differentials. Accordingly, socialists would want to make it very clear that having greater income differentials would be at the cost of failing to satisfy the needs of people who are doing all in their power to legitimately satisfy their own needs. The knowledge that this is the case should provide the more talented members of a society with the moral incentive to oppose greater income differentials, or so socialists would argue. And if some people failed to respond to this moral incentive, socialists would contend that they would be justified in forcefully requiring them to make whatever contribution is necessary so that the needs of everyone can be met.

By combining moral and self-interested reasons in this fashion, socialists hope to be able to motivate people to make their best contribution to society. In their appeal to moral incentives, however, socialists are no different from welfare liberals or libertarians, since all recognize enforceable moral constraints on the pursuit of self-interest. Disagreement between them concerns not the existence of such constraints but rather concerns their nature and how they should be enforced.

Socialists also contend that only by socializing the means of production can they effectively get people to contribute according to their ability while distribution proceeds according to need. In advanced capitalist societies, a degree of democratic control has already been extended to national defense, police and fire protection, income redistribution, and environmental protection. Socialists simply propose to extend this process of democratic control to include control of the means of production on the grounds that the very same arguments that support democratic control in these recognized areas also support democratic control of the means of production.[5] In addition, socialists contend that without such control, the means of production will be concentrated in the hands of a few, who will use those means to benefit themselves at the expense of the needs of others.

So much then for a characterization of the socialist ideal. Let us now consider how such an ideal relates to a guaranteed social minimum. Would socialists support a guaranteed social minimum? Obviously, they would. But socialists would also want to claim that such a minimum does not go far enough so as to provide for people's nonbasic needs as well as for their basic needs. They would also criticize welfare liberalism for not requiring the restructuring of jobs and socialization of the means of production.[6]

It is also important to notice that a socialist ideal of equality does not accord with what existed, until recently, in the Soviet Union.[7] Judging the acceptability of a socialist ideal by what took place in countries like the Soviet Union, where national planning was pursued without worker control, would be just as unfair as judging the acceptability of a welfare liberal ideal by what still takes place in countries like South Korea or Guatemala, where citizens are arrested and imprisoned without cause. By analogy, it would be like judging the merits of college football by the way Vanderbilt's or Columbia's team plays rather than by the way Penn State's or Notre Dame's team plays. Actually, a fairer comparison would be to judge the socialist ideal by what takes place in countries like Sweden, and to judge the welfare liberal ideal by what takes place in the United States. But even these comparisons are not quite appropriate since none of these countries fully conforms with these ideals.

DEFENSES OF THE SOCIALIST IDEAL

From Marx to the present, defenders of the socialist ideal have frequently supported their view by attacking nonsocialist ideals that most closely resemble it. The favored strategy has been to show that these ideals are inadequate in ways their defenders should have been able to recognize. Utilizing this approach, C. B. Macpherson argues that the right to self-development endorsed by both welfare liberals and socialists is only compatible with a socialist ideal of equality.[8] According to Macpherson, capitalism encourages people to acquire the power to extract benefit from others, even when this extractive power is acquired at the expense of the self-development of those over whom the power is exercised. So under capitalism, the extractive power of some is said to be increased at the expense of the developmental power of others. And while those whose extractive power is increased usually do experience an increase in developmental power as well, Macpherson claims, a net loss of developmental power still results.

It is not enough for welfare liberals to show that the transfer of power under capitalism allows for greater self-development than was possible under previous politico-economic systems. For the relevant goal is maximal self-development and only with the elimination of all extractive power under a socialist ideal, Macpherson claims, can that goal be reached.

The major difficulty with Macpherson's defense of socialism is that he does not sufficiently consider whether the right to self-development endorsed by socialists might not itself be justifiably limited by a right to liberty. In his discussion of alternative conceptions of liberty, Macpherson does criticize various formulations of negative liberty favored by libertarians, but in the main he simply endorses a conception of positive liberty that entails a right to self-development. Macpherson never tries to meet libertarians on their own terms and show that even given a reasonable construal of their own ideal, a right to liberty would naturally lead to a right to self-development.

As one might expect, there have been other attempts to defend socialism that appeal more directly to an ideal of liberty. Carol Gould regards socialism as rooted in a conception of positive liberty understood as "the fullest self-realization of social individuals."[9] According to Gould, the socialist ideal "refers to social relations in which no agents deprive any others of the conditions of their positive freedom." Since every individual has a capacity for self-realization simply by virtue of being human, Gould argues that no individual has more of a right to the conditions needed for the fulfillment of this capacity than any other. Thus, an equal right to positive liberty or freedom is said to be at the heart of the socialist ideal. Such a right, Gould argues, requires among other things, an equal access to the means of production, and, hence, is incompatible with capitalism.

Kai Nielson adopts a similar approach to defending socialism.[10] To justify the ideal of equality, Nielson argues that it is required by liberty or at least by a fair distribution of liberty. By "liberty" Nielson means both "positive liberty to receive certain goods" and "negative liberty not to be interfered with," so his argument from liberty will not have much weight with libertarians, who only value negative liberty.[11] Rather, his argument is directed primarily at welfare liberals, who value both positive and negative liberty as well as a fair distribution of liberty.

Unfortunately, neither Gould nor Nielson sufficiently takes into account the challenge to the socialist ideal from defenders of negative liberty. Both seem content to point out that defenders of negative liberty usually ignore or misrepresent the ideal of positive liberty. Yet, neither gives any compelling reason why defenders of negative liberty should recognize the requirements of socialism.

Probably the most novel of recent defenses of the socialist ideal is that set forth by Michael Walzer.[12] According to Walzer, the socialist ideal of equality requires the absence of domination, which, in turn, requires that different social goods be distributed

> for different reasons in accordance with different procedures by different agents and that all these differences derive from different understandings of the social goods.[13]

Walzer claims that our understanding of social goods such as money, education, political power, welfare, and honor requires a plurality of principles of distribution constituting autonomous "spheres of justice." In particular, Walzer argues that welfare and security should be distributed according to a shared understanding of people's needs, which vary over time and between societies.[14] He also argues that the sphere of democratic control extends not only to cities and towns but also to firms and factories because any reason that can be given for claiming that cities and towns should be subject to democratic control (rather than ownership) is also a reason for claiming that firms and factories should be subject to democratic control (rather than owner-ship).[15] Walzer contends that as long as the spheres of justice are kept distinct so that no particular social good dominates over other social goods, inequalities with respect to particular social goods, like money or honor, will not give rise to injustices. In this way, Walzer claims to have shown that while the socialist ideal of equality requires indus-trial democracy and distribution according to need, it is not opposed to certain forms of inequality.

HUMAN NATURE AS A SOCIAL PRODUCT

One issue that has continued to divide defenders of socialism is the degree to which their ideal assumes that human nature is a social prod-uct—that is, to what degree what we are is due to nurture rather than nature. Christian Bay relies minimally on this assumption.[16] He grounds his defense of socialism on what he takes to be three broad classes of universal basic human needs. First, there are physical needs, including subsistence needs and the need to be protected against vio-lence. Second, there are community needs, such as the need for self-esteem, dignity, and social recognition. Last, there are subjectivity needs, the needs we have to develop ourselves to the limits fixed by the material conditions and capabilities of the time. According to Bay, physical needs have priority over community needs, which, in turn, have priority over subjectivity needs; yet, when possible, the satisfac-tion of all three classes of basic needs is required by the socialist ideal.

By contrast, Milton Fisk relies heavily on the assumption that human nature is a social product (that is, the product of nurture), since he recognizes only a narrower class of universal basic needs, those for food, sex, support, and deliberation.[17] Furthermore, Fisk claims that these universal basic needs have no priority over those needs that are socially produced by the groups to which one belongs. It follows that for Fisk, moral principles cannot arbitrate many of the conflicts that exist (for example, between workers and owners) because such con-flicts cannot be resolved without curtailing the realization of the socially produced needs of one or the other group.

A basic difficulty with Fisk's view is that it would seemingly allow that the exploited could have socially produced needs that morally required them to submit to their exploiters. To rule out this possibil-ity, Fisk assumes that the group morality of the exploited will always require them to reject any "imposed needs" whose satisfaction

would lead to such submission. However, this would only occur if
human beings had a universal need to avoid all forms of domination,
and this is just what Fisk denies.

One reason that Fisk is reluctant to ground his socialist ideal on universal basic needs is that he thinks that moral principles must be
action-guiding in a very strong sense. Thus, in order for there to be
moral principles grounded on universal basic needs, Fisk thinks that
there must be some expectation that all rational agents will act on
those principles. Since normally all that we can expect is that rational
agents will tend to abide by conventional norms that serve the needs
of the particular groups to which they belong, Fisk concludes that
there are no universally binding moral principles.

Yet by limiting applicable moral standards to those that are action-
guiding in this very strong sense, Fisk's view deprives the exploited of
an important tool for changing their society, namely, the possibility of
morally condemning their exploiters. For even if such condemnation
is not successful in producing a change of heart in the exploiters, it still
may inspire the exploited and their allies to press for needed reforms.
So here again it seems that an ethics without universally binding
moral principles can work against the interests of the exploited.

Even so, the view that there are no universally binding moral principles is still widely endorsed by defenders of socialism.[18] This is because
the socialist ideal is not thought to be appropriate for all times and
places. Rather, the ideal is thought to be appropriate only when social
conditions have sufficiently developed to make the ideal of equality of
need-fulfillment feasible. The greatest achievement of capitalism, socialists argue, is that it has created just those social conditions in which it is
now appropriate to apply the socialist ideal. The expansion of productive forces under capitalism has now, for the first time, made it possible
to fulfill the socialist ideal of equality of need-fulfillment.

It needs to be pointed out, however, that those who claim that
there are universally binding moral principles also hold that their
practical requirements are different for different social conditions.
They claim that social conditions are relevant in two ways to the
determination of the particular requirements of morality. First, social
conditions are said to determine what sort of opportunities are available to agents both individually and collectively for fulfilling the
particular requirements of morality. For example, the available technology determines the productive capacities of different individuals
and societies. Second, social conditions are said to significantly
determine the knowledge and beliefs agents bring to the opportunities that are available to them. For example, given the ignorance and
false beliefs that pervade our understanding of sexist practices in

today's society, it is quite difficult for some people to come to appreciate the opportunities that are available to rid society of such practices. And unless agents have access to the appropriate knowledge and beliefs along with the appropriate opportunities, it will not be correct to say that morality demands that they behave in some specific manner, or at least it will not be correct to say that under such conditions they are blameworthy for failing to behave as morality demands. So it would seem that those who endorse universally binding moral principles might well grant that the application of these principles is relative to particular social conditions in much the same way as socialists claim.

Of course, there remains the question of the degree to which human nature is a social product, that is, to what degree what we are is due to nurture. Yet, the significance of this question depends on the degree to which the socialist ideal of equality can be reconciled with other social and political ideals. For if the practical requirements of the socialist ideal can be largely reconciled with the practical requirements of alternative social and political ideals, then the question of the degree to which human nature is a social product would clearly have little practical import.

WELFARE LIBERALISM AND SOCIALISM: A PRACTICAL RECONCILIATION

As we have seen, socialists endorse a guaranteed minimum, but they do not think that such a minimum goes far enough. In addition, socialists maintain that we are required to meet nonbasic needs and to socialize the means of production. Nevertheless, I shall argue that once we see how demanding the requirements of a welfare liberal ideal are (1) the additional requirement to meet nonbasic needs will be seen to have little application and (2) the additional requirement to socialize the means of production will be seen to be morally unnecessary.

The Requirement to Meet Nonbasic Needs

In support of the first contention, recall that in Chapter 2, I argued that welfare liberalism not only requires that a guaranteed minimum be provided in our own society, but also requires that we take what steps we can to provide both the same minimum to the needy in other societies as well as the resources that will be required so that future generations will be able to meet their basic needs. This social minimum was specified in terms of the satisfaction of people's basic needs. According to this standard, people are guaranteed the goods and resources necessary to meet the normal costs of satisfying their basic needs in the society in which they live. While granting that this way of specifying a social minimum introduces variation into the costs of satisfying such needs, I argued that the practice of utilizing increasingly more efficient means of satisfying people's basic needs in developed societies would appear to have the effect of equalizing the normal costs of meeting people's basic needs across societies. More significantly still, I argued that in order to meet the basic needs of existing and future generations, the scope of the satisfaction of nonbasic needs would have to be drastically limited. As a consequence, once we distribute goods and resources in accordance with a welfare liberal ideal so as to meet the basic needs of existing and future generations, there should be very little left over for the satisfaction of nonbasic needs as a socialist ideal requires.

However, this way of reconciling welfare liberal and socialist ideals has been challenged by Michael Walzer.[19] Walzer contends that especially in the international arena, we lack a set of common meanings or shared values to ground the rights of distant peoples and future generations to have their basic needs satisfied. On Walzer's view, we have shared values when we are strongly motivated to act upon those values, or, as he would put it, when those values are actually reflected in our choices.[20] Since there is no general tendency among people in affluent societies to recognize a right to a social minimum for distant peoples and future generations, Walzer contends that we lack the shared values to ground such a right.

But why should the existence or justification of specific rights depend upon a general tendency among people to respect those rights? Obviously, no one would deny that it is easier to get people to respect specific rights if they already have the propensity to do so. But even when people lack the propensity, they still can be brought to respect specific rights by educational or coercive means, provided they still have the capacity to do so. Thus, in order to get people to respect specific rights all that is absolutely necessary is that they have the capacity to respect those rights; it is not necessary that they presently have the propensity to do so as well.

In fact, provided that people have the capacity to respect specific rights, what is most relevant to the justification of those rights are the reasons that can be given for or against actualizing that capacity. This is not to deny that people's propensities for respecting specific rights are not also relevant in this regard. Yet, because these propensities may be ill-formed or underdeveloped in various ways, they are never by themselves decisive with respect to the justification of such rights. That is why in giving the justification of the welfare rights of distant peoples and future generations in Chapter 2, I implicitly assumed that people had the capacities for respecting such rights, and I simply sought to show that such rights were required by the welfare liberal ideal of fairness. I argued that when judged from the perspective of the original position, the satisfaction of the basic needs of existing and future generations has precedence over the satisfaction of nonbasic needs, even when most people presently lack the propensity (but not the capacity) to respect this priority. What I am now claiming is that because the welfare rights of distant peoples and future generations can be supported in this fashion, it is possible to practically reconcile the welfare liberal ideal of fairness and the socialist ideal of equality.

But what about Walzer's own attempt to reconcile these two ideals? As we noted earlier, Walzer argues that welfare and security should be distributed on the basis of need and that the sphere of democratic control extends not only to cities and towns but also to firms and factories. Yet clearly, these arguments would not have much force if they required that people presently have the propensity (and not just the capacity) to act in accord with their premises. However, if we evaluate the arguments in terms of how compelling they are from a welfare liberal perspective, they do seem to have considerable force, and they would be even more forceful still if in order to take into account the welfare rights of distant peoples and future generations, we restricted their scope to basic needs and interests. But to do that is simply to combine Walzer's argument with the previous argument for reconciling the welfare ideal and socialist ideals.

Now it should be pointed out that while this argument for practical reconciliation does not assume that people presently have the propensity to respect the welfare rights of distant peoples and future generations, the absence of that propensity does create a practical problem. The problem is how to get people to respect those rights. It is a problem of incentive, and it seems to me that its solution must rely heavily upon moral incentives. People have to be strongly motivated on *moral grounds* to produce according to their ability so that everyone's basic needs can be met. Such a solution requires that once people realize that their most fundamental social and political ideals demand respect for the welfare rights of distant peoples and future generations, a sufficient number of them should be willing to take the steps to acquire the appropriate propensities in this regard. If a sufficient number are willing, then, it would be possible to bring others into conformity by educational or coercive means.

Of course, to some extent it may be possible to rely upon self-interested incentives to motivate the more talented. This would involve making jobs as intrinsically rewarding as possible as well as offering greater income to the more talented to get them to use their talents fully. But any inequalities of income must be kept limited if everyone's basic needs are to be met. This is because despite the fact that it is theoretically possible to have significant income differentials while respecting the welfare rights of distant peoples and future generations, practically, because of limited goods and resources, this will not obtain. Hence, the only morally adequate solution to the problem of incentive is to limit income differentials, make jobs as intrinsically rewarding as possible, and then rely heavily upon moral incentives to get people to produce according to their ability in order that everyone's basic needs can be met.

I submit, therefore, that once we distribute resources in accordance with a welfare liberal ideal so as to meet the basic needs of distant peoples and future generations, there would be very few goods and resources left over for the satisfaction of nonbasic needs. Of course, the scope of the requirements of a welfare liberal ideal has not always been appreciated; yet once it is taken into account, the further requirement of a socialist ideal of equality to meet nonbasic needs as well, can be seen to have little application.

The Requirement to Socialize the Means of Production

We have seen that in order to meet everyone's basic needs it is necessary to introduce limited income differentials, make jobs more intrinsically rewarding, and rely heavily upon moral incentives to get people to produce according to their ability. But is it necessary to go further and to socialize the means of production? I contend that it would suffice to simply distribute control over goods and resources more widely. Presently, in the United States 10 percent of families own 57 percent of the total net wealth and 86 percent of total financial assets, and 0.5 percent owns 19 percent of the total net wealth and 34 percent of total financial assets.[21] In the 1980s in the United States, the average pretax income of families in the top 1 percent increased by 77 percent while income to the bottom 20 percent fell by 9 percent.[22]

Accordingly, to meet people's basic needs in the United States, it would surely be necessary to change that distribution at least to some degree. Also, to meet people's basic needs worldwide, it would be necessary to adopt more efficient means for meeting people's basic needs in affluent societies generally. Clearly, there are more efficient ways of meeting people's basic nutritional needs than using so much grain to feed livestock at such a tremendous loss of usable protein. But since all of these requirements for meeting people's basic needs already follow from a welfare liberal ideal, I conclude that there is no need to adopt the socialist ideal's additional requirement to socialize the means of production. This additional requirement is morally unnecessary given the demands of a welfare liberal ideal.

As Marx pointed out, the widespread exploitation of laborers associated with early capitalism only began when large numbers "had
been robbed of all their own means of production and of all the guarantees of existence afforded by the old feudal system" by persons and
economic groups who already had considerable wealth and power.[23]
But the concentration of wealth and power necessary to carry out such
exploitation is not likely to be found in a society that in accordance
with a welfare liberal ideal provides for the basic needs of all its members as well as for the basic needs of distant peoples and future
generations. By restricting private ownership of the means of production in this way, all the morally necessary steps toward socializing the
means of production would have thereby been taken.

Approaching the issue in yet another way, it seems clear that for
Marx socializing the means of production is best construed as a means
to an end. The end for Marx would be to form "an association in which
the free development of each is the condition of the free development
of all."[24] But then the question arises as to why this end cannot be adequately pursued by widely dispersing the ownership of the means of
production.

It might be argued that to bring about such an association would
require that individuals be given control over their working conditions (or have the option of controlling those conditions). For
example, Barry Clark and Herbert Gintis contend that "strengthen-
ing the system of total liberties" requires such worker control and
would lead to the abolition of capitalism.[25] Yet, even supposing that
an appropriate degree of worker control were required to form an
association in which the free development of each is the condition of
the free development of all,[26] why would not such worker control be
compatible with a system in which the ownership of the means of
production were widely dispersed throughout the society? Under
such a system, individuals *as investors* would each decide how to
invest the fairly small shares of capital they owned. Thus, some
would want to invest in firms in which they worked so that their
own productivity would contribute to a return on their investment.
Others would choose not to do so, realizing that they could get a
higher return from their investment if they invested their shares of
capital elsewhere. Over such investment decisions, however, individuals *as workers* would have no control. But once these decisions
had been made, then the rights of individuals as workers would
have to be taken into account in designing the business enterprise.

Suppose a group of investors decide to form a firm, call it
Proletarians United, to produce superwidgets, believing that many
people would love to have one. Under a system of worker control, the
workers that Proletarians United employs would have to be guaran-

teed significant control over such features of their working conditions
as job descriptions; working hours; and hiring, firing, and promotion
policies. Further, it would not be possible under the proposed system
for Proletarians United to extract an unfair advantage from the workers it employs by threatening to replace them with other workers. The
reason for this is that as long as the demands for worker control are
reasonable and allow for a good return on their investment, workers
under the proposed system normally would either be able to find
other firms willing to employ them or be able to pool their own investment holdings and go into business for themselves. Thus, even
granting that a welfare liberal ideal would require a significant degree
of worker control, this requirement would still seem to be perfectly
compatible with a system that permitted a certain degree of differential control of the means of production.

This is not to deny that there would be a need for some degree of
democratic control of the flow of investment to ensure that individuals as consumers would be able to satisfy their basic needs, but again
such control would seem to be perfectly compatible with a system
that permitted a certain degree of differential control of the means of
production.

Furthermore, given that socialists grant that some income differentials would be necessary to motivate people to make their best
contribution to society, how then can they object to similar differentials in the control of the means of production if these differentials
would also serve to motivate people to make their best contribution to
society? As long as such differentials are kept within limits as they
necessarily must be if the basic needs of distant peoples and future
generations are to be met, then what objection could socialists have to
such differentials?

Of course, socialists might contend that allowing any differentials in
the control of the means of production would be unstable and would
eventually lead to greater differentials over time with adverse consequences for the general welfare, but it is difficult to see why this is a
serious threat. Both a system which allows some differential control of
the means of production and a system which allows only uniform control could be subverted by those who occupy important positions of
leadership and authority, but it is difficult to see how a system with
differential control is any more likely to be subverted. In fact, a system
with limited differential control may be less likely to be subverted
since it is better able to motivate people to make their best contribution to society.

In brief, I have argued that as soon as we recognize how demanding
the requirements of a welfare liberal ideal are, the socialist's additional
requirement to socialize the means of production can be seen to be

morally unnecessary. Of course, it might be objected that, given the highly exploitative character of modern capitalism, it would be best to pave the way for the drastic reform or revolution that is needed by proclaiming the need to socialize the means of production. This may be. But then it may also be best to pave the way for the drastic reform or revolution that is needed by appealing to those frequently endorsed, but rarely understood, moral requirements of a welfare liberal ideal. At the very least, the latter approach cannot be faulted for failing to appeal to a morally adequate social and political ideal.

LEGITIMATE AUTHORITIES AND THE IDEAL OF EQUALITY

What remains to be considered is whether the socialist's ideal of equality can justify coercive institutions as legitimate authorities. As we noted in our discussion of the welfare liberal ideal, once we consider the degree of redistribution that would be necessary to achieve a guaranteed social minimum within our own society and in the world at large, it is hard to see how coercive institutions would not be required. Likewise, as we noted before, the degree to which coercive institutions would be required would depend on the level and type of opposition that existed to achieving a guaranteed social minimum. Fortunately, a major problem with providing a justification for coercive institutions now seems closer to a resolution. This is because the welfare liberal ideal of fairness, the libertarian ideal of liberty, and the socialist ideal of equality can now be seen to be reconcilable at the practical level because they all require a right to a social minimum. The welfare liberal ideal requires, as we have seen, a basic-needs social minimum, and there is every reason to think that the libertarian ideal of liberty requires the same. Furthermore, as we have seen in this chapter, providing such a minimum both within one's society and to distant peoples and future generations goes a long way toward reconciling the welfare liberal ideal and the libertarian ideal with the socialist ideal of equality.

What remains to be seen, however, is whether the practical reconciliation that we have found among the welfare liberal, socialist, and libertarian ideals can be extended to other ideals, like the feminist, the communitarian, and multicultural ideals, that we will be considering, respectively, in the next three chapters. If it can be extended, it seems clear that we will be able to justify coercive institutions that support a basic-needs minimum. But if we cannot achieve a practical reconciliation with these other ideals, the task of providing a justification for coercive institutions will not have been successfully completed.

Notes

1. Eugene Debs was the Socialist party's presidential candidate in 1904, 1908, 1912, and from jail in 1920, but one would probably not call him a viable candidate.

2. Karl Marx, *Critique of the Gotha Program*, ed. by C. P. Dutt (London, International Publishers, 1966).

3. For a discussion of worker control, see David Schweickart, *Capitalism or Worker Control?* (New York, Praeger, 1980); Branko Horwat, *The Political Economy of Socialism* (Armonk, 1982); and Carole Pateman, *Participation and Democratic Theory* (New York, Cambridge University Press, 1970).

4. Edward Nell and Onora O'Neill, "Justice under Socialism," in *Justice: Alternative Political Perspectives*, 2d ed., ed. James P. Sterba (Belmont, CA: Wadsworth, 1991).

5. Means of production are goods not used for direct human consumption but rather to produce other goods.

6. For reasons why a social program that guarantees a right to welfare does not appear to go far enough, see John H. Schaar, "Equality of Opportunity and Beyond," in *Equality*, ed. by Roland Pennock and John Chapman (New York, New York University Press, 1967).

7. Until recently in the Soviet Union, achieving the socialist ideal was subordinated to maintaining central control over (potentially) rebellious republics and peoples and competing in an expensive arms race with the United States.

8. C. B. Macpherson, *Democratic Theory* (London, Oxford University Press, 1973).

9. Carol Gould, *Marx's Social Ontology* (Cambridge, MIT Press, 1978).

10. Kai Nielson, *Equality and Liberty* (Totowa, NJ: Rowman & Littlefield, 1985).

11. The libertarian ideal of negative liberty is discussed in Chapter 3.

12. Michael Walzer, *Spheres of Justice* (New York, Basic Books, 1983).

13. *Ibid.*, 6.

14. *Ibid.*, Chapter 3.

15. *Ibid.*, 291–303.

16. Christian Bay, *Strategies of Political Emancipation* (Notre Dame, University of Notre Dame Press, 1981).

17. Milton Fisk, *Ethics and Society* (New York, New York University Press, 1980).

18. In addition to Fisk's work, see Steven Lukes, *Essays in Social Theory*, (New York, New York University Press, 1977), Parts 2 and 3, and William Ash, *Morals and Politics* (London, Routledge, 1977).

19. Walzer, especially Chapter 1.

20. *Ibid.*, 5. In reaching this understanding of Walzer's view, I have profited from Norman Daniels's review of Walzer's book in *Philosophical Review* (1985), 142–148.

21. Federal Reserve Board, "Financial Characteristics of High-Income Families," *Federal Reserve Bulletin* (Washington, D.C., December 1986),

164–177. Richard Parker, *The Myth of the Middle Class* (New York: Harper & Row, 1972), 212.

22. *New York Times* (March 5, 1992).

23. Karl Marx, *Capital*, vol. 1 (New York, International Publishers, 1967), 715.

24. Karl Marx and Friedrich Engels, *Communist Manifesto* (New York: International Publishers), 47.

25. Barry Clark and Herbert Gintis, "Rawlsian Justice and Economic Systems," *Philosophy and Public Affairs* (1978), 312–313.

26. For considerations that favor worker control, see Harry Braveman, *Labor and Monopoly Capitalism* (New York, 1974); Carole Pateman, *Participation and Democratic Theory* and *Work in America* (Cambridge, MIT Press, 1973); and Clark and Gintis, 302–325.

5

Feminism: The Ideal of Androgyny

Contemporary feminists almost by definition seek to put an end to male domination and to secure women's liberation. To achieve these goals, many feminists support the social and political ideal of a gender-free or androgynous society.[1] According to these feminists, all assignments of rights and duties are ultimately to accord with the ideal of a gender-free or androgynous society.

But how is this ideal to be interpreted? A gender-free or genderless society is one where basic rights and duties are not assigned on the basis of a person's biological sex. Being male or female is not the grounds for determining what basic rights and duties a person has in a gender-free society. But this is to characterize the feminist ideal only negatively. It tells us what we need to get rid of, not what we need to put in its place. A more positive characterization is provided by the ideal of androgyny. According to this ideal, the traits that are truly desirable in society should be equally open to both women and men, or in the case of virtues, equally expected of both women and men. So characterized, the ideal of androgyny represents neither a revolt against so-called feminine virtues and traits nor their exaltation over so-called masculine virtues and traits.[2] Putting the feminist ideal more positively in terms of the ideal of androgyny also helps to bring out why men should be attracted to feminism.

DEFENSES OF ANDROGYNY

There are various contemporary defenses of the ideal of androgyny. Some feminists have attempted to derive the ideal from a welfare liberal ideal of fairness. Others have attempted to derive the ideal from a socialist ideal of equality. Let us briefly consider each of these defenses in turn.

In Chapter 2, our discussion of a welfare liberal ideal focused on the right to a basic-needs minimum and the application of this right to distant peoples and future generations. Such a right, however, as derived from a welfare liberal ideal of fairness (or even from a libertarian ideal of liberty if our previous argument for practical reconciliation holds) also entails a right to equal opportunity—that is, a right not to be discriminated against in filling the roles and positions in society. It is this right to equal opportunity that feminists have tended to focus on in attempting to derive the ideal of androgyny from a welfare liberal ideal.[3] Of course, equal opportunity could be interpreted minimally as providing people only with the same legal rights of access to all advantaged positions in society for which they are qualified. But this is not the interpretation given the right by welfare liberals. In a welfare liberal ideal, equal opportunity is interpreted to require in addition the same prospects for success for all those who are relevantly similar, where relevant similarity involves more than simply present qualifications. For example, Rawls claims that persons in his original position would favor a right to "fair equality of opportunity," which means that persons who have the same natural assets and the same willingness to use them would have the necessary resources to achieve similar life prospects.[4] The point feminists have been making is simply that failure to achieve the ideal of androgyny translates into a failure to guarantee equal opportunity to both women and men.

The support for the ideal of androgyny provided by a socialist ideal of equality appears to be much more direct than that provided by a welfare liberal ideal of fairness.[5] This is because the socialist ideal and the ideal of androgyny can be interpreted as requiring the very same equal right of self-development. What a socialist ideal purports to add to this interpretation of the ideal of androgyny is an understanding of how the ideal is best to be realized in contemporary capitalist societies. For according to advocates of this socialist defense of androgyny, the ideal is best achieved by socializing the means of production and satisfying people's nonbasic as well as their basic needs. Thus, the general idea behind this approach to realizing the ideal of androgyny is that a cure for capitalist exploitation will also be a cure for women's oppression.

FEMINIST OBJECTIONS

In her recent book *Justice, Gender and the Family*, Susan Okin also examines the capacity of a welfare liberal ideal to support the ideal of a gender-free society, which I take to be the same as an androgynous society.[6] Noting Rawls's failure to apply his original position-type thinking to family structures, Okin is skeptical about the possibility of using a welfare liberal ideal to support a feminist ideal of a gender-free or androgynous society. She contends that in a gender-structured society like our own, male philosophers cannot achieve the sympathetic imagination required to see things from the standpoint of women. In a gender-structured society, Okin claims, male philosophers cannot do the original position-type thinking required by a welfare liberal ideal because they lack the ability to put themselves in the position of women. So, according to Okin, original position-type thinking can only really be achieved in a gender-free or androgynous society.

Yet at the same time that Okin despairs of doing original position-type thinking in a gender-structured society, like our own, she herself purportedly does a considerable amount of just that type of thinking. For example, she claims that Rawls's principles of justice "would seem to require a radical rethinking not only of the division of labor within families but also of all the nonfamily institutions that assume it."[7] She also claims that "the abolition of gender seems essential for the fulfillment of Rawls's criterion of political justice."[8]

But which is it? Can we or can we not do the original position-type thinking required by a welfare liberal ideal of fairness? I think that Okin's own work, and the work of others, demonstrates that we can do such thinking and that her reasons for thinking that we cannot are not persuasive. To do original position-type thinking, it is not necessary that everyone be able to put themselves imaginatively in the position of everyone else. All that is necessary is that some people be able to do so. For some people may not be able to do original position-type thinking because they have been deprived of a proper moral education. Others may be able to do original position-type thinking only after they have been forced to mend their ways and live morally for a period of time.

Moreover, in putting oneself imaginatively in the place of others, one need not completely replicate the experience of others; for example, one need not actually feel what it is like to be a murderer to adequately take into account the murderer's perspective. Original position-type thinking with respect to a particular issue only requires a general appreciation of the benefits and burdens that accrue to people affected by that issue. So, to achieve a feminist ideal, we need to be able to generally appreciate what women and men stand to gain and lose when moving from a nonandrogynous or gendered society to an androgynous or gender-free society.

Of course, even among men and women in our gendered society who are in a broad sense morally capable agents, some may not presently be able to do such original position-type thinking with respect to the proper relationships between men and women; these men and women may only be able to do so after the laws and social practices in our society have significantly shifted toward a more gender-free society. But this inability of some to do original position-type thinking does not render it impossible for others, who have effectively used the opportunities for moral development available to them to achieve the sympathetic imagination necessary for original position-type thinking with respect to the proper relationships between men and women. Accordingly, Okin has not provided any compelling reason to reject our previous argument that a welfare liberal ideal of fairness supports the ideal of androgyny.

APPLYING THE IDEAL

One locus for the radical restructuring required by the ideal of a gender-free or androgynous society is the family. Here two fundamental changes are needed. First, all children, irrespective of their sex, must be given the same type of upbringing consistent with their native capabilities. Second, mothers and fathers must normally also have the same opportunities for education and employment consistent with their native capabilities.[9]

Yet, at least in the United States, this need to radically modify traditional family structures to guarantee equal opportunity confronts a serious problem. Given that a significant proportion of the available jobs are at least 9 to 5, families with preschool children require day-care facilities if their adult members are to pursue their careers. Unfortunately, for many families such facilities are simply unavailable. In New York City, for example, more than 144,000 children under the age of six are competing for 46,000 full-time slots in day-care centers. In Seattle, there is licensed day-care space for 8,800 of the 23,000 children who need it. In Miami, two children, three and four years old, were left unattended at home while their parent worked. They climbed into a clothes dryer while the timer was on, closed the door, and burned to death.[10]

Moreover, even the available day-care facilities are frequently inadequate either because their staffs are poorly trained or because the child/adult ratio in such facilities is too high. At best, many such facilities provide little more than custodial care; at worst, they actually retard the development of those under their care.[11] What this suggests is that at least under present conditions, if preschool children are to be adequately cared for, frequently one of the adult members of the family has to remain at home to provide that care. But because most jobs are at least 9 to 5, this requires that the adult members who stay at home temporarily give up pursuing a career. However, such sacrifice appears to conflict with the equal opportunity requirement of a feminist ideal.

Families might try to meet this equal opportunity requirement by having one parent give up pursuing a career for a certain period of time and the other give up pursuing a career for a subsequent (equal) period of time. But there are problems here too. Some careers are difficult to interrupt for any significant period of time, while others never adequately reward latecomers. In addition, given the high rate of divorce and the inadequacies of most legally mandated child support, those who first sacrifice their careers may find themselves later faced with the impossible task of beginning or reviving their careers while continuing to be the primary caretaker of their children.[12] Furthermore, there is considerable evidence that children benefit more from equal rearing from both parents.[13] So the option of having just one parent doing the child rearing for any length of time is, other things being equal, not optimal.

It would seem therefore, that to truly share child-rearing within the family what is needed is flexible (typically part-time) work schedules that allow both parents to be together with their children for a significant period every day. Some flexible job schedules have already been tried by various corporations.[14] But if equal opportunity is to be a reality in our society, the option of flexible job schedules must be guaranteed to all those with preschool children. Some estimates show that married full-time career women spend an average of 3.8 hours per day on housework while married full-time career men spend an average of .7 hour per day.[15] Obviously, this will have to change if we are to achieve the ideal of a gender-free or androgynous society.

A second locus of change required by the ideal of a gender-free or androgynous society is the distribution of economic power in the society. In the United States, the percentage of women in the labor force has risen steadily for three decades, from 35 percent (of those aged sixteen or more) in 1960 to 58 percent in 1992. Roughly 72 percent of women were employed in 1990, including more than 58 percent of mothers with children under the age of six and 53 percent of mothers with children under the age of one.[16]

Yet, in 1991 women employed full time still earned $.70 for every $1 men earned, up from the $.60 for every $1 that held from the 1960s through the 1980s. Earnings do increase with education for all workers, but women and men of color earn less than white men at every level of education. For example, women with four years of college education earn less on average than men who have not completed high school.[17]

Sometimes women and men working in the same job category have different incomes. For example, while female secretaries earned a median wage of $278 per week in 1985, the median wage for male secretaries was $365.[18] More frequently, however, women and men tend to be employed in different job categories that are paid differently. According to one study done a few years ago in the state of Washington, women employed as clerk-typists earned less than men employed as truck drivers or warehouse workers. In another study done in Denver, women employed as nurses earned less than men employed as tree cutters. While in each of these cases, the women earned about 20 percent less than the men, the women's jobs when evaluated in terms of skill, responsibility, effort, and working conditions were given equal or higher scores than the men's jobs with which they were compared. Clearly, denying women the opportunity to earn the same as men do for equal or comparable work is a basic injustice in our society, and it will be a very costly one to correct.[19]

It is sometimes assumed that the problem of unequal pay for comparable work will be solved once women move into male-dominated occupations.[20] Unfortunately, as the feminization of certain occupations occurs, we are seeing a subsequent drop in pay for men. For example, as the percentage of women bartenders increased 23 points, men's pay dropped 16 percent and as the percentage of women pharmacists increased 12 points, men's pay fell 11 percent.[21] So the discrimination against women in the economic arena is a far more entrenched problem than is sometimes thought.

The problem assumes even greater proportions when we consider the world at large. According to a United Nations report, although women are responsible for 66 percent of all work produced in the world (paid and unpaid) they receive only 10 percent of the salaries.[22] The same report shows that men own 99 percent of all the property in the world, and women only 1 percent. Clearly, we have a long way to go to achieve the equality required by a feminist ideal of a gender-free or androgynous society.

It is also important to recognize that the equality required by a feminist ideal cannot be achieved on men's terms. It is not an equality in which men's values prevail and women's values are lost. As an example of what needs to be avoided, consider the integration of Girl Scouts and Boy Scouts into the same troops in Norway.[23] Before integration, many women had been troop leaders of the Girl Scouts, but after the integration, almost all troops were led by men and the former women leaders became assistant leaders. In addition, an analysis of the activities in the former Girl Scouts compared to the activities of the former Boy Scouts revealed that the activities of the girls were of a more cooperative nature than those of the boys. The boys had activities in which they competed more against each other or against other groups of boys. After integration, the competitive activities of the boys became the activities of both girls and boys. The cooperative activities of the girls were abandoned. The integration was made on the boys' terms.[24]

But a feminist ideal is not a one-way street. If it is to be achieved, each person who is capable must be expected to have the virtues that are now typically associated with women (for example, nurturance, caring, sensitivity, compassion) as well as virtues that are now typically associated with men (for example, self-reliance, courage, decisiveness).

To remedy these inequalities suffered by women in the economic arena will require programs of affirmative action and comparable worth. Affirmative action is needed to place qualified women into positions they deserve to occupy because of past discrimination. Without affirmative action, the structural violence of past discrimination will not be rectified. Only with affirmative action can the competition for desirable jobs and positions be made fair again given our history of past discrimination. There are even cases where affirmative action candidates are clearly the most qualified; nevertheless, those in charge of hiring, because of their prejudice, could only see the candidates as simply qualified, but not the most qualified candidates.[25]

Comparable worth is also needed because, without it, women will not receive the salaries they deserve. They will do work that is judged equal or comparable to the work that men are doing in male-dominated occupations, but, without comparable worth, they will be paid less than men are being paid. Paying for comparable worth programs will not be easy. A settlement in the state of Washington granted nearly $500 million to women workers in order to achieve pay equity.[26] Even larger settlements are anticipated as Canada begins to implement extensive comparable worth programs.[27]

A third locus of change required by the ideal of a gender-free or androgynous society is the overt violence perpetrated against women in our society. "The home is actually a more dangerous place for the American woman than the city streets," according to former Surgeon General Antonia Novello. "One-third of the women slain in the U.S.," she continues, "die at the hands of husbands and boyfriends."[28] In addition, women in the United States live in fear of rape. Forty-four percent of women are raped according to a recent study, and almost 50 percent of male college students say they would commit rape if they were certain that they could get away with it.[29] Not infrequently, women are beaten by their own husbands and lovers (between one quarter and one third of women are battered in their homes by husbands and lovers).[30] One third of all women who require emergency room hospital treatment are there as a result of domestic violence.[31] Thirty-eight percent of little girls are sexually molested inside or outside the family.[32] Since most of these crimes are minimally prosecuted in our society, women in our society can be raped, battered, or sexually abused as a child and little, if anything, will be done about it. What this shows is that the condition of women in our society is actually that of being subordinate to men, by force.

To see that this problem is not confined to the United States, S. Opdebeeck reports that 40 percent of Belgian women between 30 and 40 years old experienced some form of physical and/or sexual family violence, and Bert Young notes that spousal assault against wives is the leading cause of homicide in Canada.[33] Obviously, this subordination of women must end if we are to achieve the ideal of a gender-free or androgynous society.

A feminist ideal requires that we put an end to the overt violence against women which takes the distinctive form of rape, battery, and sexual abuse. This overt violence is in every way as destructive as the other forms of violence we oppose. So we cannot in consistency fail to oppose this form of violence done to women in our society. According to one cross-cultural study of ninety-five societies, 47 percent of them were free of rape.[34] What this shows is that it is possible to eliminate, or, at least, to reduce drastically, overt violence against women.

One way to help bring about this result is to ban hard-core pornography that celebrates and legitimizes rape, battery, and the sexual abuse of children, as the Supreme Court of Canada has just recently done.[35] Catharine MacKinnon has argued that pornography of this sort causes harm to women by increasing discriminatory attitudes and behavior in men toward women that takes both violent and nonviolent forms.[36]

Another way to decrease violence against women is to deemphasize violent sports like boxing and football. To see why this would help, all one needs to do is consider the evidence. For example, an exhaustive study of heavyweight prizefights held between 1973 and 1978 and subsequent homicide statistics showed that homicides in the United States increased by over 12 percent directly after heavyweight championship prizefights. In fact, the increase was greatest after heavily publicized prizefights.[37] In addition, a study of 24 cases of campus gang rapes indicated that 9 of them were by athletes, and in an investigation of sexual assaults on college campuses which included interviewing over 150 campus police, it turned out that football and basketball players were involved in 38 percent of the reported cases.[38] There is also a 40 percent increase in batteries by husbands and boyfriends associated with the yearly Superbowl football game. In the Chicago area, a local radio station went so far as to recommend that women "take a walk" during the game in order to avoid being assaulted in their homes.[39]

A third way to help reduce violence against women is to teach conflict resolution, child care, and the history of peacemaking in our schools. Several schools have experimented with teaching conflict resolution and child care to grade and high school children with impressive results, especially for boys.[40] The history of peacemaking could also provide our children with a new and better set of models than the history of war-making has done.[41]

SEXUAL HARASSMENT

Another locus of change required by the ideal of a gender-free or androgynous society overlaps the previous two. It is rooted in the distribution of economic power in society and it frequently takes the form of overt violence against women. It is the problem of sexual harassment, and, given its importance, we will devote some time to discussing it.

Actually, sexual harassment was not recognized as an offense by U.S. trial courts until the late 1970s, and it was only affirmed by the U.S. Supreme Court as an offense in the 1980s. The term *sexual harassment* was not even coined until the 1970s. So the moral problem of sexual harassment is one that many people have only recently come to recognize. The Senate Judiciary Committee hearings on Anita Hill's charge that Clarence Thomas had sexually harassed her obviously heightened people's awareness of this problem.

According to various studies done over the last few years, sexual harassment is a widespread problem. In research done by psychologists, 50 percent of women in the workplace questioned said they had been sexually harassed. According to the U.S. Merit Systems Protection Board, within the federal government, 56 percent of 8,500 female workers surveyed claimed to have experienced sexual harassment. According to the *National Law Journal*, 64 percent of women in "pink-collar" jobs reported being sexually harassed and 60 percent of 3,000 women lawyers at 250 top law firms said that they had been harassed at some point in their careers. In a recent survey by *Working Women* magazine, 60 percent of high-ranking corporate women said they have been harassed; 33 percent more knew of others who had been.[42]

According to Ellen Bravo and Ellen Cassedy, humiliation is the term most commonly used by those who see themselves as sexually harassed to describe their experience.[43] They see themselves as demeaned and devalued, and treated as sexual playthings. Many find themselves in a double bind. If they fight, they could lose their jobs or alienate their boss or co-workers. If they don't fight, they could lose their self-respect. Many experience stress-related ailments—depression, sleep or eating disorders, headaches, and fatigue—and take more days off from work as a result.[44]

The economic consequences for employers are also significant. A 1988 survey of 160 large manufacturing and service companies found this startling result: a typical Fortune 500 company with 23,750 employees loses $6.7 million per year because of sexual harassment. And this loss doesn't even include lawsuits. What it does include are financial losses due to absenteeism, lower productivity, and employee turnover. Another 1988 study showed that sexual harassment cost the federal government $267 million between 1985 and 1987. It cost $37 million to replace federal workers who left their jobs, $26 million in medical leave due to stress from sexual harassment, and $204 million in lost productivity.[45]

Given the seriousness of the problem, it is important to get clear about what constitutes, or should constitute, sexual harassment. In 1980, the Equal Employment Opportunity Commission (EEOC) issued guidelines finding harassment on the basis of sex to be a violation of Title VII of the Civil Rights Act of 1964, and defining sexual harassment as "unwelcome sexual advances, requests for sexual favors, and other verbal or physical conduct of a sexual nature" when such behavior occurred in any of three circumstances:

1. where submission to such conduct is made either explicitly or implicitly a term or condition of an individual's employment,

2. where submission to or rejection of such conduct by an individual is used as the basis for employment decisions affecting the individual, or

3. where such conduct has the purpose or effect of unreasonably interfering with an individual's work performance or creating an intimidating, hostile, or offensive working environment.[46]

In 1986, the U.S. Supreme Court in *Meritor Savings Bank* v. *Vinson* agreed with the EEOC, ruling that there could be two types of sexual harassment: harassment that conditions concrete employment benefits on granting sexual favors (often called the quid pro quo type) and harassment that creates a hostile or offensive work environment without affecting economic benefits (the hostile environment type).[47]

Nevertheless, the Supreme Court made it difficult for a plaintiff to establish that either of these types of sexual harassment had occurred. For example, a polite verbal "no" does not suffice to show that sexual advances are unwelcome; a woman's entire conduct both inside and outside the workplace is subject to appraisal to determine whether or not she welcomed the advances. In the Vinson case, there was "voluminous testimony regarding Vinson's dress and personal fantasies," and in the Senate Judiciary Committee hearings, Anita Hill was not able to prevent intensive examination of her private life, although Clarence Thomas was able to declare key areas of his private life as off-limits, such as his practice of viewing and discussing pornographic films.

The Supreme Court also made it difficult to classify work environments as hostile to women unless the harassment is sufficiently severe or pervasive. Applying the Supreme Court's standard, a lower court, in *Christoforou* v. *Ryder Truck Rental*, judged a supervisor's actions of fondling a plaintiff's rear end and breasts, propositioning her, and trying to force a kiss at a Christmas party to be "too sporadic and innocuous" to support a finding of a hostile work environment.[48] Similarly, in *Rabidue* v. *Osceola Refining Co.*, a workplace where pictures of nude and scantily clad women abounded, including one, which hung on a wall for eight years, of a woman with a golf ball on her breasts and a man with his golf club, standing over her and yelling "fore," and where a co-worker, never disciplined despite repeated complaints, routinely referred to women as "whores," "cunts," "pussies," and "tits," was judged by a lower court not to be sufficiently hostile an environment to constitute sexual harassment.[49] Notice, *by contrast*, that the Senate Arms Services Committee, in its recent hearings, regarded an environment in which known homosexuals are simply doing their duty in the military to be *too hostile* an environment to ask particularly male heterosexuals to serve in.

Yet why should we accept the Supreme Court's characterization of sexual harassment, especially given its unwelcomeness and pervasiveness requirements?[50] As the Supreme Court interprets sexual harassment, a person's behavior must be unwelcome in a fairly strong sense before it constitutes sexual harassment. But why should a woman have to prove that an offer "If you don't sleep with me you will be fired" is unwelcome before it constitutes sexual harassment? Isn't such an offer objectively unwelcome? Isn't it just the kind of offer that those in positions of power should not be making to their subordinates—offers that purport to make their continuing employment conditional upon providing sexual favors? Surely, unless we are dealing with some form of legalized prostitution, such offers are objectively unwelcome.[51]

Given, then, that such offers are objectively unwelcome, why is there any need to show that they are also subjectively unwelcome before regarding them as violations of Title VII of the Civil Rights Act? The requirement of subjective unwelcomeness is simply a gratuitous obstacle, which makes the plaintiff's case far more difficult to prove than it should be.[52]

In addition, if the plaintiff is fired after refusing such an offer, the Supreme Court requires the plaintiff to prove that the firing occurred because the offer was refused, which is very difficult to do, unless one is a perfect employee. Wouldn't it be fairer, then, to require the employer to prove that the plaintiff would have been fired even if she had said "yes" to the offer. Of course, employers could avoid this burden of proof simply by not making any such offers in the first place.[53] But when they do make objectively unwelcome offers, why shouldn't the burden of proof be on them to show that any subsequent firing was clearly unrelated to the plaintiff's refusal. Fairness is particularly relevant in this context because we are committed to equal opportunity in the workplace, which requires employing women and men on equal terms. Accordingly, we must guard against imposing special burdens on women in the workplace, when there are no comparable burdens imposed on men. A feminist ideal of a gender-free or androgynous society will be satisfied with nothing less.[54]

The demand for equal opportunity in the workplace also appears to conflict with the Supreme Court's pervasiveness requirement for establishing a hostile environment. Citing a lower court, the Supreme Court contends that to be actionable, sexual harassment "must be sufficiently severe or pervasive 'to alter the conditions of the [victim's] employment and create an abusive working environment.'"[55] But as this standard has been interpreted by lower courts, the pervasiveness of certain forms of harassment in the workplace has become grounds for tolerating them. In *Rabidue*, the majority argued

> [i]t cannot seriously be disputed that in some work environments, humor and language are rough hewn and vulgar. Sexual jokes, sexual conversations and girlie magazines abound. Title VII was not meant to— or can—change this. Title VII is the federal court mainstay in the struggle for equal employment opportunity for the female workers of America. But it is quite different to claim that Title VII was designed to bring about a magical transformation in the social mores of American workers.[56]

The Supreme Court itself seems to sound a similar theme by emphasizing the application of Title VII to only extreme cases of sexual harassment as found in *Vinson*.

However, as the EEOC interprets Title VII, the law has a broader scope. Title VII affords employees the right to work in an environment free from discriminatory intimidation, ridicule, and insult. According to the EEOC, sexual harassment violates Title VII where conduct creates an intimidating, hostile, or offensive environment or where it unreasonably interferes with work performance.[57]

But how are we to determine what unreasonably interferes with work performance? In *Rabidue*, the majority looked to prevailing standards in the workplace to determine what is reasonable or unreasonable. Yet Justice Keith, in dissent, questioned this endorsement of the status quo, arguing that just as a Jewish employee can rightfully demand a change in her working environment if her employer maintains an anti-Semitic work force and tolerates a workplace in which "kike" jokes, displays of Nazi literature, and anti-Jewish conversation "may abound," surely women can rightfully demand a change in the sexist practices that prevail in their working environments.[58] In *Henson v. Dundee*, the majority also drew an analogy between sexual harassment and racial harassment:

Sexual harassment which creates a hostile or offensive environment for members of one sex is every bit the arbitrary barrier to sexual equality at the workplace that racial harassment is to racial equality. Surely, a requirement that a man or woman run a gauntlet of sexual abuse in return for the privilege of being allowed to work and make a living can be as demeaning and disconcerting as the harshest of racial epithets.[59]

And this passage is also quoted approvingly by the Supreme Court in *Vinson*.

Moved by such arguments, the majority in *Ellison* v. *Brady* proposed that rather than look to prevailing standards to determine what is reasonable, we should look to the standard of a reasonable victim, or given that most victims of sexual harassment are women, the standard of a reasonable woman.[60] They contend that this standard may be different from the standard of a "reasonable man." For example, what male superiors may think is "harmless social interaction" may be experienced by female subordinates as offensive and threatening.[61]

Nevertheless, if we are concerned to establish the equal opportunity in the workplace that a feminist ideal of a gender-free or androgynous society demands, there should be no question about what standard of reasonableness to use here. It is not that of a reasonable woman nor that of a reasonable man for that matter, but the standard of what is reasonable for everyone to accept. For equal opportunity is a moral requirement, and moral requirements are those that are reasonable for everyone to accept. This assumes that apparent conflicts over what is reasonable to accept (for example, conflicts between the standard of a reasonable woman and the standard of a reasonable man) are conflicts that can and should be resolved by showing that one of these perspectives is more reasonable than the other, or that some still other perspective is even more reasonable. However, at least in the context of sexual harassment, this standard of what is reasonable for everyone to accept will accord closely with the standard of a reasonable woman, given that once women's perspectives are adequately taken into account, the contrasting perspective of a reasonable man will be seen as not so reasonable after all.

In its decision in *Harris* v. *Forklift* (1993), the Supreme Court took an important step toward a more reasonable stance on sexual harassment. In this case, Teresa Harris worked as a rental manager at Forklift Systems. Charles Hardy, Forklift's president, told Harris on several occasions, in the presence of other employees, "You're a woman, what do you know?" and "We need a man as the rental manager." Again in front of others, he suggested that the two of them "go to the Holiday Inn to negotiate (Harris's) raise." Hardy occasionally asked

Harris and other female employees to get coins from his front pants pockets. On other occasions, he threw objects on the ground in front of Harris and other women, and asked them to pick the objects up. He made sexual innuendoes about Harris's and other women's clothing. On one occasion, while Harris was arranging a deal with one of Forklift's customers, Hardy asked Harris in front of other employees, "What did you do, promise . . . some (sex) Saturday night?" Soon after Harris quit her job at Forklift.

In this case, the Supreme Court struck down the district court's requirement that in order for sexual harassment to be established, Harris needed to show that Hardy's conduct had "seriously affected her psychological well-being." This was an important decision, but obviously it does not go far enough in establishing a reasonable standard for sexual harassment.

In this chapter, I have argued that a feminist ideal of a gender-free or androgynous society requires a number of important changes in our society. It requires changes in the family, particularly, equal socialization for girls and boys, and equal opportunity for mothers and fathers. It requires changes in the distribution of economic power in our society through programs of affirmative action and comparable worth that remove the structural violence against women. It requires changes that are necessary to put an end to the overt violence against women that takes the form of rape, battery, and sexual abuse. Last, it requires changes that implement new programs against sexual harassment in the workplace in order to achieve the equal opportunity that a feminist ideal promises to everyone.

Given that a feminist ideal of a gender-free and androgynous society has roots in a welfare liberal ideal of fairness and a socialist ideal of equality (and also in a libertarian ideal of liberty if our previous argument for practical reconciliation holds), then it would seem that those who are committed to any of these social and political ideals should have no difficulty accepting these practical requirements of a feminist ideal once they come to see that these requirements are also the practical requirements of the social and political ideals to which they are committed.

LEGITIMATE AUTHORITIES AND THE IDEAL OF ANDROGYNY

Now that it is clear that a feminist ideal of a gender-free and androgynous society is rooted in the welfare liberal, socialist, and libertarian ideals, the task of justifying particular coercive institutions as legitimate authorities seems closer to completion. The practical reconciliation of these ideals shows that they will not end up endorsing different coercive institutions as legitimate authorities. We still need to determine, however, whether that agreement can be extended to include the ideals of communitarianism and multiculturalism. We also need to determine whether the coercive institutions that are justified according to these ideals are any of the coercive institutions under which we now live or only some other type of coercive institutions yet to be established in the future. If the former, we who endorse these ideals will know which existing coercive institutions to obey. If the latter, our goal with respect to existing coercive institutions would be to replace them by whatever means are morally permissible. This extremely practical issue will be taken up in Chapter 8.

Notes

1. See, for example, Ann Ferguson, "Androgyny as an Ideal for Human Development," in *Feminism and Philosophy*, ed. Mary Vetterling-Braggin et al. (Totowa, NJ: Rowman and Littlefield, 1977), 45–69; Mary Ann Warren, "Is Androgyny the Answer to Sexual Stereotyping?" in *"Femininity," "Masculinity," and "Androgyny,"* ed. Mary Vetterling-Braggin (Totowa, NJ: Rowman and Littlefield, 1982), 170–186; A. G. Kaplan and J. Bean, eds., *Beyond Sex-Role Stereotypes: Reading Toward a Psychology of Androgyny* (Totowa, NJ: Rowman and Littlefield, 1976); Andrea Dworkin, *Women Hating* (New York, Dutton, 1974), Part IV; Carol Gould, "Privacy Rights and Public Virtues: Women, the Family and Democracy," in *Beyond Domination*, ed. Carol Gould, (Totowa, NJ: Rowman and Littlefield, 1983), 3–18; Carol Gould, "Women and Freedom," *The Journal of Social Philosophy* (1984): 20–34; Linda Lindsey, *Gender Roles* (Englewood Cliffs, NJ: Prentice Hall, 1990); and Marilyn Friedman, "Does Sommers Like Women?" *Journal of Social Philosophy* (1991): 75–90. For some feminists who oppose the ideal of androgyny, see Mary Daly, *Gyn-Ecology: The Meta-Ethics of Radical Feminism* (Boston, Beacon, 1978); Kathryn Paula Morgan, "Androgyny: A Conceptual Critique," *Social Theory and Practice* (1982); and Jean Bethke Elstain, "Against Androgyny," *Telos* 47 (1981).

2. For a valuable discussion and critique of these two viewpoints, see Iris Young, "Humanism, Gynocentrism and Feminist Politics," *Women's Studies International Forum* 8, no. 3 (1985): 173–183.

3. See, for example, Virginia Held, *Rights and Goods* (New York, Free Press, 1984), especially Chapter 11; Gloria Steinem, "What It Would Be Like If Women Win," *Time* (August 31, 1970): 22–23; and Mary Jeanne Larrabee, "Feminism and Parental Roles: Possibilities for Changes," *Journal of Social Philosophy* 14 (1983): 18. See also National Organization for Women (NOW) Bill of Rights, and *Statement on the Equal Rights Amendment*, United States Commission on Civil Rights (1978).

4. John Rawls, *A Theory of Justice* (Cambridge, Harvard University Press, 1971), 73.

5. See, for example, Ann Ferguson, "Androgyny as an Ideal for Human Development," in *Feminism and Philosophy*, ed. Mary Vetterling-Braggin et al. and Evelyn Reed, "Women: Caste, Class or Oppressed Sex?" in *Morality in Practice*, ed. James P. Sterba (Belmont, CA: Wadsworth, 1983), 222–228.

6. Susan Okin, *Justice, Gender and the Family* (New York, Basic Books, 1989), Chapter 5.

7. *Ibid.*, 104.

8. *Ibid.*, 104.

9. The reason for qualifying this claim is that mothers and fathers, unlike children, may legitimately waive their right to equal opportunity when the reasons are compelling enough.

10. *New York Times* (November 25, 1987).

11. *Ibid.* See also Phyllis Moen, *Woman's Two Roles* (New York, Auburn House, 1992).

12. Lenore Weitzman, *The Divorce Revolution: The Unexpected Social and Economic Consequences for Women and Children in America* (New York, Free Press, 1985).

13. Dorothy Dinnerstein, *The Mermaid and the Minotaur* (New York, Harper & Row, 1977); Nancy Chodorow, *Mothering: Psychoanalysis and the Sociology of Gender* (Berkeley, University of California Press, 1978); and Vivian Gornick, "Here's News: Fathers Matter as Much as Mothers," *Village Voice* (October 13, 1975).

14. *New York Times* (November 27, 1987).

15. Birgit Brock-Utne, *Educating for Peace* (New York, Pergamon, 1985), 6–7.

16. *The New York Times* (October 6, 18, and 19, 1992). See also Moen, *Woman's Two Roles.*

17. Elaine Sorensen, "The Comparable Worth Debate," in *Morality in Practice*, 4th ed., ed. James P. Sterba (Belmont, CA: Wadsworth, 1993).

18. Okin, *Justice*, Chapter 7.

19. Jerry Jacobs and Ronnie Steinberg, "Compensating Differentials and the Male-Female Wage Gap," *Social Forces* 69, no. 2 (December 1990).

20. Clifford Hackett, "Comparable Worth: Better from a Distance," *Commonweal* (May 31, 1985).

21. *Rapid City Journal* (October 20, 1992).

22. Report on the World Conference of the United Nations Decade for Women, Copenhagen, 14–30 July 1981.

23. Birgit Brock-Utne, 100–101

24. Similarly, Deborah Tannen contends that when men and women get together in groups, they are likely to talk in ways more familiar and comfortable to men. See Deborah Tannen, *You Just Don't Understand* (New York, Morrow, 1990).

25. Gertrude Ezorsky, *Racism and Justice* (Ithaca, NY: Cornell University Press, 1991).

26. Ellen Paul, *Equity and Gender* (New Brunswick, NJ: Sage Publications, 1989), 83. By 1987, 10 states had implemented some form of pay equity policies and 27 states and 166 localities had begun comparable worth studies. Among states that have taken action, Minnesota has most completely adopted and implemented a comparable worth scheme for public employees. See Mary Ann Mason, "Beyond Equal Opportunity: A New Vision for Women Workers," *Notre Dame Journal of Law, Ethics and Public Policy* (1992), 403.

27. *Financial Post* (March 3, 1990).

28. *New York Times* (October 17, 1991).

29. Catherine MacKinnon, *Feminism Unmodified* (Cambridge, Harvard University Press, 1987) and Bert Young, "Masculinity and Violence," presented at the Second World Congress on Violence and Human Coexistence, Montreal, 12–17 July 1992.

30. MacKinnon.

31. Dierdre English, "Through the Glass Ceiling," *Mother Jones* (November 1992).

32. MacKinnon.

33. S. Opdebeeck, "Determinants of Leaving an Abusing Partner," presented at the Second World Congress on Violence and Human Coexistence, Montreal, 12–17 July 1992 and Young, "Masculinity."

34. Myriam Miedzian, *Boys Will Be Boys* (New York, Anchor Books, 1991), 74.

35. *Donald Victor Butler* v. *Her Majesty the Queen*.

36. MacKinnon.

37. David Phillips, "The Impact of Mass Media Violence on U.S. Homicides," *American Sociological Review* (1983): 560–568.

38. Miedzian, 203–204.

39. WBBM, January 31, 1993. Playing football also impacts negatively on the life expectancies of football players themselves. The average life expectancy of National Football League players in the United States is 54, nearly two decades below the overall male mean. See Don Sabo, "Sport, Patriarchy and Male Identity," *The Arena Review* (1985): 1–30.

40. *Ibid.*, Chapters 6 and 7.

41. Duane Cady, *From Warism to Pacifism* (Philadelphia, Temple University Press, 1989), Chapter 1 and Birgit Brock-Utne, *Feminist Perspectives on Peace and Peace Education* (New York, Pergamon, 1989) 162–163.

42. Cherly Gomez-Preston, *When No Means No* (New York: Carol Publishing Co., 1993), 35–36. Ellen Bravo and Ellen Cassedy, *The 9-5 Guide to Combating Sexual Harassment* (New York, John Wiley & Sons, 1992), 4–5. The problem is international as well. A three-year study of women in Estonia, Finland, Sweden, and the Soviet Union showed that nearly 50 percent of all working women in these countries experienced sexual harassment. A survey released in 1991 by the Santama Group to Consider Sexual Harassment at Work showed that about 70 percent of Japanese women say they have experienced some type of sexual harassment on the job. See Susan Webb, *Step Forward* (New York: Master Media, 1991), xiv, xvii.

43. Bravo and Cassedy, 43ff.

44. *Ibid.*

45. *Ibid.*, 49–50.

46. "EEOC 1980 Guidelines on Sexual Harassment" in *Fair Employment Practices, Labor Relations Reporter*, The Bureau of National Affairs, Inc.

47. *Meritor Savings Bank* v. *Vinson*, 477 U.S. 57, 106 S. Ct. 2399, 91 L.Ed. 49 (1983).

48. *Christoforou* v. *Ryder Truck Rental*, 668 F. Supp. 294 (S.D.N.Y. 1987).

49. *Rabidue* v. *Osceola Refining Co.*, 805 F.2d 611, 620 (6th Cir. 1986).

50. In a recent study, Barbara A. Getek determined that a number of factors influence whether people tend to classify certain behavior as sexual harassment. They are:

1. how intrusive and persistent the behavior (the more physically intrusive and persistent the behavior is, the more likely that it will be defined as sexual harassment).

2. the nature of the relationship between the actors (the better the actors know each other, the less likely the behavior will be labeled sexual harassment).

3. the characteristics of the observer (men and people in authority are less likely to label behavior as sexual harassment).

4. the inequality in the relationship (the greater the inequality, the more likely the behavior will be labeled sexual harassment).

Barbara Getek, "Understanding Sexual Harassment at Work," *Notre Dame Journal of Law, Ethics and Public Policy* (1992).

51. Even where there is legalized prostitution, such offers may still be objectively unwelcome.

52. There is an analogous requirement of subjective consent in the law concerning rape that is similarly indefensible. See Susan Estrich, "Sex at Work," *Stanford Law Review* (1991).

53. Or they could simply not fire those to whom they make the conditions.

54. Barbara Getek contends that sexual harassment is caused by the fact that women are stereotypically identified as sexual objects in ways that men are not. She notes that women are stereotypically characterized as sexy, affectionate, and attractive, whereas men are stereotypically characterized as competent and active. These stereotypes, Getek claims, spill over into the workplace, making it difficult for women to be perceived as fellow workers rather than sex objects, and it is these perceptions that foster sexual harassment ("Understanding Harassment"). It would seem, therefore, that eliminating the problem of sexual harassment from our society will require breaking down these stereotypes. But this, of course, is just what the ideal of a gender-free or androgynous society hopes to do.

55. *Meritor Savings Bank* v. *Vinson*, 67.

56. *Rabidue* v. *Osceola.*

57. "EEOC 1980 Guidelines."

58. *Rabidue.*

59. *Henson* v. *Dundee*, 682 F.2d 897, 904 (11th Cir. 1982).

60. *Ellison* v. *Brady*, 924 F.2d 872 (9th Cir. 1991).

61. As one of Getek's studies shows, reasonable men and reasonable women can disagree over what constitutes sexual harassment in the workplace. In this study, 67.2 percent of men as compared to 16.8 percent of women would be flattered if asked to have sex, while 15 percent of men and 62.8 percent of women said they would be insulted by such an offer ("Understanding Harassment").

6

Communitarianism: The Ideal of the Common Good

Virtually all political philosophers pay at least lip service to the ideal of the common good but only communitarians take the ideal to be the fundamental social and political ideal. There are two reasons for this. First, communitarians take a conception of the right to be based on a conception of the good. Second, communitarians see the common good as constituted by the practices of communities. The common good is the good that is internal to the practices of communities. So as communitarians it is fitting that they should give pride of place to the common good.

As one might expect, many contemporary defenders of communitarianism regard their view as rooted in Aristotelian moral theory. Yet, many contemporary defenders of communitarianism also agree with Alasdair MacIntyre that if Aristotelian moral theory is to be rationally acceptable it must be refurbished in certain respects. Specifically, MacIntyre claims that Aristotelian moral theory must, first, reject any reliance on a metaphysical biology.[1] Instead, MacIntyre proposes to ground Aristotelian moral theory on a conception of a practice. A practice, for MacIntyre, is "any coherent and complex form of socially established cooperative human activity through which goods internal to that form of activity are realized in the course of trying to achieve those standards of excellence which are appropriate to and partially definitive of that form of activity, with the result that human powers to achieve excellence, and human conceptions of the ends and goods involved are systematically extended."[2] As examples of practices, MacIntyre cites arts, sciences, games, and the making and sustaining of family life.[3]

MacIntyre then partially defines the virtues in terms of practices. A virtue, such as courage, justice, or honesty, is "an acquired human quality the possession and exercise of which tends to enable us to achieve those goods which are internal to practices and the lack of which prevents us from achieving any such goods."[4] However, MacIntyre admits that the virtues that sustain practices can conflict (for example, courage can conflict with justice) and that practices so defined are not themselves above moral criticism.[5]

Accordingly, to further ground the communitarian account, MacIntyre introduces the conception of a telos or good of a whole human life conceived as a unity.[6] It is by means of this conception that MacIntyre proposes to morally evaluate practices and resolve conflicts between virtues. For MacIntyre, the telos of a whole human life is a life spent in seeking that telos; it is a quest for the good human life and it proceeds with only partial knowledge of what is sought. Nevertheless, this quest is never undertaken in isolation but always within some shared tradition.[7] Moreover, such a tradition provides additional resources for evaluating practices and for resolving conflicts while remaining open to moral criticism itself.

MacIntyre's characterization of the human telos in terms of a quest undertaken within a tradition marks a second respect in which he wants to depart from Aristotle's view. This historical dimension to the human telos that MacIntyre contends is essential for a rationally acceptable communitarian account is absent from Aristotle's view.

By refurbishing Aristotle's view in these ways, MacIntyre hopes to avoid the radical disagreement, interminable arguments, and incommensurable premises that he claims characterize contemporary moral philosophy.[8] These three features, MacIntyre claims, are illustrated in the contemporary debate between Robert Nozick and John Rawls.[9] Nozick argues for the libertarian view that principles of just acquisition and exchange set limits on the possibility of achieving certain distributive goals. According to Nozick, if the outcome of the application of the principles of just acquisition and exchange is severe inequalities in distribution, the toleration of such inequalities is the price to be paid for justice. By contrast, Rawls argues for the welfare liberal view that principles of just distribution set limits on the possibilities for acquisition and exchange. According to Rawls, if the outcome of the application of the principles of just distribution interferes with previous acquisition and exchange, the toleration of such interference is the price to be paid for justice.

This Nozick-Rawls debate has engaged defenders on both sides, and certainly the debate has been characterized by radical disagreement and interminable arguments. But MacIntyre further claims that the debate proceeds from incommensurable premises. According to MacIntyre, Rawls's view is ultimately based on the principle that

people's basic needs should be met, whereas Nozick's view is ultimately based on the principle that people should be able to keep what
they legitimately acquire or earn, and these two principles, MacIntyre
contends, cannot be rationally weighed against each other, and, hence,
are incommensurable.[10]

MacIntyre claims that this sad state of affairs in which contemporary moral philosophy finds itself has its origin in the
Enlightenment of the seventeenth and the eighteenth centuries. As
MacIntyre tells the story, key philosophers of that period, such as
David Hume and Immanuel Kant, attempted to provide a rational
justification for morality while rejecting Aristotelian moral theory.
These philosophers began with a conception of human nature as it
is and attempted to derive therefrom a justification for adhering to
everyday moral precepts. They attempted to show that some
feature or features of human nature as it is would lead persons to
endorse those everyday moral precepts. To ground morality, Hume
appealed to human passions and Kant to human reason.

But, MacIntyre argues that these attempts to ground morality not
only failed but had to fail because by rejecting an Aristotelian conception of human nature as it should be and appealing only to
human nature as it is, these attempts deprived themselves of just
what was needed to ground everyday moral precepts. According to
MacIntyre, it is the failure of these attempts to justify morality from
the Enlightenment to the present that has led to the current
predicament in contemporary moral philosophy. The only way out
of this predicament, MacIntyre claims, is for contemporary moral
philosophy to return to Aristotelian moral theory, the rejection of
which has brought contemporary moral philosophy to its current
sorry state.

DEFENSES OF THE IDEAL

Communitarians have frequently chosen to defend their view by
attacking other views, and, by and large, they have focused their
attacks on welfare liberalism.

One of the best-known attacks of this sort has been put forth by
Michael J. Sandel.[11] What Sandel claims is that welfare liberalism is
founded upon an inadequate conception of the nature of persons,
according to which none of the particular wants, interests, or ends that
we happen to have at any given time constitute who we are essentially. According to this conception, we are independent of and prior
to all such wants, interests, or ends. As Sandel points out, this conception of the nature of persons is similar in certain respects to Kant's
doctrine of transcendental subjects of experience. Yet contemporary
welfare liberals, like Rawls, would not be particularly happy with the

comparison since they have attempted to give their conception an empirical rather than a transcendental foundation.

Sandel claims that what is inadequate about this conception of the nature of persons is that

> we cannot regard ourselves as independent in this way without great cost to those loyalties and convictions whose moral force consists partly in the fact that living by them is inseparable from understanding ourselves as the particular persons we are—as members of this family or community or nation or people, as bearers of this history, as sons and daughters of that revolution, as citizens of this republic. Allegiances such as these are more than values I happen to have or aims I "espouse at any given time." They go beyond the obligations I voluntarily incur and the "natural duties" I owe to human beings as such. They allow that to some I owe more than justice requires or even permits, not by reason of agreements I have made but instead in virtue of those more or less enduring attachments and commitments which taken together partly define the person I am.[12]

Thus, according to Sandel, the conception of the nature of persons required by welfare liberalism is inadequate because it fails to take into account the fact that some of our wants, interests, and ends are at least in part constitutive of who we are essentially. Without these desires, interests, and ends, we would not be the same persons we presently happen to be.

Sandel contends that welfare liberals are led to rely upon this inadequate conception of persons for reasons that are fundamental to the social and political ideals they want to defend. Specifically, welfare liberals want to maintain the priority of justice and more generally the priority of the right over the good. For example, according to Rawls:

> The principles of right and so of justice put limits on which satisfactions have value; they impose restrictions on what are reasonable conceptions of one's good. We can express this by saying that in justice as fairness the concept of right is prior to that of the good.[13]

To support these priorities, Sandel argues that welfare liberals are led to endorse this inadequate conception of the nature of persons. For example, Rawls argues:

> It is not our aims that primarily reveal our nature but rather the principles that we would acknowledge to govern the background conditions under which these aims are to be found and the manner in which they are to be pursued. *For the self is prior to the ends which are affirmed by it;*

even a dominant end must be chosen from among numerous possibilities. . . . We should therefore reverse the relation between the right and
the good proposed by teleological doctrines and view the right as
prior.[14]

What this passage shows, according to Sandel, is that for welfare liberals, like Rawls, the priority of justice and the priority of the right are
grounded in the priority of the self to its ends.

Furthermore, Sandel argues that welfare liberals are also led to rely
upon this inadequate conception of the nature of persons because they
believe that people's native assets should be regarded as common assets
on the grounds that no one deserves her or his particular set of native
assets. In order to show, therefore, that regarding native assets as common
assets does not violate the Kantian injunction never to treat persons
merely as means, Sandel claims that welfare liberals are required to conceive of persons as distinct from their assets so that while their assets may
be used simply as a means, they themselves would never be so used.

But, according to Sandel:

> The notion that only my assets are being used as a means, not me, threat-
> ens to undermine the plausibility, even the coherence, of the very
> distinction it invokes. It suggests that . . . we can take seriously the distinc-
> tion between persons only by taking metaphysically the distinction
> between a person and his attributes. But this has the consequence of
> leaving us with a subject so shorn of empirically-identifiable characteristics,
> . . . as to resemble after all a Kantian transcendent or disembodied subject.[15]

Yet, this is just the result that contemporary defenders of welfare liberalism had hoped to avoid.

If communitarianism is to be reconciled with our other four conceptions of justice, it is necessary to show that (1) contrary to what
Alasdair MacIntyre claims, contemporary moral philosophy is not
characterized by radical disagreement, interminable arguments, and
incommensurable premises; (2) the particular communitarian objections to welfare liberalism raised by Michael J. Sandel can be
answered; and (3) communitarianism does not impose practical
requirements that are significantly different from those that are
imposed by our other social and political ideals. Let us see whether it
is possible to establish each of these claims in turn.

THE STATE OF CONTEMPORARY MORAL PHILOSOPHY

According to MacIntyre, the only way to avoid the radical disagreement, interminable arguments, and incommensurable premises that

characterize contemporary moral philosophy is to adopt a communitarian perspective based on an Aristotelian moral theory that has been refurbished in at least two respects. First, the theory would have to abandon any reliance on a metaphysical biology. Second, it would have to characterize the human telos in terms of a quest undertaken within a tradition.

But how would an Aristotelian moral theory that has been refurbished in these ways help us to avoid the radical disagreement, interminable arguments, and incommensurable premises that MacIntyre claims characterize contemporary moral philosophy. MacIntyre says little about the particular practices and tradition that, according to his theory, are to ground an account of the virtues. But without a specification of these practices and tradition, and the virtues that are grounded upon them, how are we to avoid the radical disagreements and interminable arguments that MacIntyre claims characterize contemporary moral philosophy?

MacIntyre does explain how his refurbished Aristotelian moral theory avoids choosing between incommensurable premises by continuing to recognize the force of the rival moral goods not chosen.[16] But why is that option not also available to defenders of other contemporary views? Surely, libertarians can show some regard for meeting basic needs provided the requirements of just appropriation and exchange have been taken into account. For example, they can recognize the goal of meeting basic needs as a requirement of supererogation.[17] Likewise, welfare liberals can show some regard for previous appropriation and exchange, at least after everyone's basic needs have been met.

Yet, the capacity of an ethical theory for recognizing the force of the rival moral goods not chosen does not suffice to show that the theory can avoid choosing between incommensurable premises. And it no more suffices in the case of MacIntyre's refurbished Aristotelian moral theory than it does in the case of other contemporary theories—virtually all of which have this same capacity. For two theories can have this capacity even when their premises are incommensurable, due to the fact that they require radically opposed priorities with respect to particular goods. For example, this would hold of Rawls's and Nozick's theories if Rawls's theory regarded the goal of meeting basic needs to be fundamentally a requirement of obligation and Nozick's theory regarded that goal to be fundamentally a requirement of supererogation.[18] Consequently, MacIntyre's proposed solution to avoiding choosing between incommensurable premises simply will not work.

What will work, I contend, is the approach that I have adopted in this book. In order to show that the premises of rival social and political ideals are not really incommensurable and that radical disagreement and interminable arguments can also be avoided, it should suffice to show that when rival social and political ideals are correctly interpreted, they can be shown to support the same practical requirements.

It is also worth noting that in his more recent work Alasdair MacIntyre has significantly qualified his commitment to the incommensurability thesis with which he is so widely associated.[19] MacIntyre now allows that while alternative social and political ideals are incommensurable, it is still possible for a sensitive interpreter to come to adequately understand competing ideals so as to raise problems for those ideals that should lead either to their abandonment or their modification. MacIntyre credits Aquinas with being a sensitive interpreter of Aristotelianism and Augustinianism who showed the need to modify each perspective to produce a more adequate synthesis. MacIntyre sees himself as being the sensitive interpreter of two views that he calls the *encyclopaedist* (which he apparently thinks contains the core view of liberalism) and the *genealogist* (which represents an ugly form of relativism). MacIntyre then attempts to show that both of these views are plagued with internal contradictions, which he takes to provide support for the Augustinian-Aristotelian synthesis that he derives from Aquinas. Obviously, welfare liberals welcome MacIntyre's newly stated recognition that it is possible to argue nonarbitrarily with respect to alternative social and political ideals. Unfortunately, the liberalism MacIntyre criticizes in this work is only a caricature of contemporary liberalism. Ironically, it turns out that contemporary liberalism, understood as the welfare liberalism we have been discussing, is in fact one variant of the general Augustinian-Aristotelian synthesis that MacIntyre derives from Aquinas!

MacIntyre has also recently argued that virtually all forms of liberalism attempt to separate rules defining right action from conceptions of the human good.[20] MacIntyre contends that these forms of liberalism not only fail but have to fail because the rules defining right action cannot be adequately grounded apart from a conception of the good. For this reason, MacIntyre claims, only some refurbished Aristotelian theory that grounds rules supporting right action in a complete conception of the good can ever hope to be adequate.

But why can't we view most forms of liberalism as attempting to ground moral rules on part of a conception of the good—specifically, that part of a conception of the good that is more easily recognized, and needs to be publicly recognized, as good? For Rawls, for example, this partial conception of the good is a conception of fairness, according to which no one deserves his or her native abilities or his or her initial starting place in society. If this way of interpreting liberalism is correct, then, in order to properly evaluate alternative social and political ideals, we would need to do a comparative analysis of their conceptions of the good and their practical requirements. However, since the conception of the good so far specified and defended by MacIntyre is actually relatively formal when compared with the conceptions developed by liberal theorists, it is difficult to know if, where, and to what extent his theory actually differs from their theories in its practical applications.

THE COMMUNITARIAN OBJECTIONS OF SANDEL

As we have seen, Sandel argues that welfare liberalism is objectionable because it is based upon an inadequate conception of the nature of persons. At first glance, Sandel's case against welfare liberalism looks particularly strong. After all, Rawls actually does say that "the self is prior to the ends which are affirmed by it" and this claim seems to express just the inadequate conception of the nature of persons that Sandel contends underlies welfare liberalism. Further, Rawls's claim is not made specifically about persons in the original position. So Sandel cannot be dismissed for failing to distinguish between the characterization of persons in the original position and the characterization of persons in ordinary life, as Rawls himself seems to suggest in a recent article.[21] Nevertheless, Sandel's case against welfare liberalism presupposes that there is no other plausible interpretation that can be given to Rawls's claim than the metaphysical one that Sandel favors. However, there does appear to be a more plausible interpretation of Rawls's claim. According to this interpretation, to say that persons are prior to their ends simply means that they are morally responsible for those ends to the degree that they can or could have changed them. Of course, the degree to which people can or could have changed their ends varies, but it is that which determines the degree to which we are morally responsible for those ends and, hence, morally prior to them.

This interpretation does not deny that certain ends may in fact be constitutive of the persons we are, so that if those ends were to change we would become different persons. We can see, therefore, that nothing in this interpretation of Rawls's claim presupposes a self that exists prior to all its ends. Rather, the picture we are given is that of a self that is responsible for its ends insofar as its ends can or could have been revised. Such a self may well be constituted by at least some of its ends, but it is only responsible for those ends to the degree to which they can or could have been revised. So the sense in which a self is prior to its ends is simply moral: insofar as its ends can or could have been revised, a self may be called upon to change them or compensate others for their effects when they turn out to be morally objectionable. Clearly, this interpretation of Rawls's claim avoids any commitment to the inadequate conception of the nature of persons which Sandel contends underlies welfare liberalism.

However, Sandel contends that welfare liberals, like Rawls, are also driven to endorse an inadequate conception of the nature of persons because they believe that people's native assets should be regarded as common assets. Sandel argues that the only way to show that regarding native assets as common assets does not violate the Kantian injunction never to treat persons merely as a means is for welfare liberals to conceive of persons as distinct from their assets, so that while their assets may be used simply as a means, they themselves would never be so used.

Obviously, in order to evaluate this objection to welfare liberalism, we must first get clear about the conditions under which the Kantian injunction never to treat people merely as a means would be violated. Only then can we determine whether, as Sandel claims, welfare liberals are required to adopt an inadequate conception of the nature of persons in order to avoid violating this Kantian injunction.[22]

Now, according to Robert Nozick, who first raised this objection to welfare liberalism, the paradigm case of being simply used is that of an exchange in which one party to the exchange does not freely accept the terms or underlying purposes of the exchange.[23] Nozick distinguishes between cases where the exchange is objectionable because one party judges the compensation provided by the other party to be inadequate (I'm being paid too little for my work), and cases where the exchange is objectionable because one party disapproves of the other party's purpose in carrying out the exchange (I don't want my retirement funds invested in exploiting Third World countries). Unfortunately, Nozick's characterization of his paradigm case is defective, and for reasons Nozick himself should have recognized.

First, exchanges that people do not freely accept, that is, forced exchanges, do not necessarily involve simply using people. For example, Nozick allows that in the absence of free agreement a dominant protection agency would be justified in prohibiting persons not protected by the agency from employing certain risky procedures provided that adequate compensation is paid by the agency to those persons.[24] And surely Nozick would not want to grant that this is a case of simply using someone. So there can be cases of forced exchanges that do not involve simply using people, even when the force is not being employed in response to any wrongful action.[25]

Second, even when people freely accept the terms and purposes of an exchange, this does not preclude their being simply used. People may freely accept the terms and purposes of an exchange only because they have been socially conditioned, against their most fundamental interests, to do so. Nancy Davis, who has pressed this particular objection against Nozick's account, provides the following example.

> The Victim is a lonely, shy, and insecure individual, while the Controller is a charismatic charmer. The Controller pays a lot of flattering attention to the Victim with the aim of getting her to become a live-in, all-purpose drudge: what he wants is someone who will attend to his domestic chores, fawn on him, and—since this is what she will be convinced that she wants to do—make no fuss about it. Even if the Victim is told that this is what the Controller wants, understands that this is really all that he wants, and agrees to take on the job of all-purpose drudge, we may still think that she is being used. Though she is not ignorant of the Controller's aims and purposes, she is (given her psychological makeup) overwhelmed by his attentions. He is thus able to exercise a strong or special influence over her.[26]

This example seems to be a clear case of a person being used even though, in her present circumstances, she has freely agreed to be so used.

So it would seem that the defining characteristics of Nozick's paradigm case of being simply used are neither necessary nor sufficient for an adequate account of that notion. People can be used even when they have freely agreed to the terms and purposes of an exchange or relationship (as in Davis's example) and people may not be used even when they are forced to agree to the terms or purposes of an exchange or relationship (as in Nozick's own example).

What is needed, therefore, to correctly characterize the conditions under which people are being simply used is some suitably idealized standpoint that is relevantly different from the one that the party happens to be in at the moment. Not surprisingly, Rawls claims that his original position can provide us with just such a standpoint.[27] According to Rawls, to avoid simply using people we need only treat them in accord with the requirements that would be chosen in the original position. On this view, whether exchanges, either forced or free, involve simply using people depends upon the requirements that would be chosen in the original position. For example, since a right to welfare would be chosen in the original position, to forcefully require people to help guarantee such a right would not violate the Kantian injunction not to treat people simply as a means. And because such a right would be chosen in the original position, the rich would, in fact, be violating that injunction in their dealings with the poor, even if the poor had freely agreed to inadequate wages as the only terms of their continued employment by the rich. Alternatively, to appease those who might find this use of Rawls's original position question-begging, we could adopt the idealized standpoint of the "ought" implies "can" principle and avoid simply using people by treating them in accord with the requirements it would be reasonable to ask everyone affected to accept.

Using either standard, it would turn out, given what has been established in previous chapters, that requiring people to use their native assets to help guarantee a right to welfare and a right to equal opportunity would not violate the Kantian injunction not to treat people simply as a means. In view of these interpretations of the Kantian injunction, therefore, there is no need to regard the self as distinct from its assets in order to avoid violating that injunction while recognizing that people are required to regard their native assets as common assets, at least insofar as people are required to use those assets to make a fair contribution toward guaranteeing a right to welfare and a right to equal opportunity. For these reasons, Sandel has failed to show that welfare liberalism is based on an inadequate conception of the nature of persons.

Sometimes, however, Sandel objects to welfare liberalism not so much because it is committed to an inadequate conception of the nature of persons but because it is neutral with respect to conceptions of the good. How, Sandel asks, can agents determine what is just independently of some conception of the good?[28] Yet, despite the fact that well-known liberals, like Rawls and Dworkin, have endorsed this characterization of welfare liberalism, it is apt to be more misleading than helpful. What it suggests is that welfare liberals are attempting to be value-neutral when they clearly are not. Welfare liberals, like their communitarian critics, are committed to a substantive conception of the good. For example, the political conception of the good that Rawls endorses rules out any complete or comprehensive conception of the good that conflicts with it.[29] It also rules out, without much argument, a libertarian conception of the good.[30] So clearly, in this respect, Rawls makes no claim to being neutral with respect to conceptions of the good. Consequently, Sandel's alternative objection to welfare liberalism fails as well because this social and political ideal, like virtually every other social and political ideal, is not truly neutral with respect to conceptions of the good.

THE PRACTICAL REQUIREMENTS OF COMMUNITARIANISM

Yet, despite the failure of Sandel's objections to welfare liberalism, there still may be significant practical differences between the requirements of communitarianism and our five other social and political ideals. In particular, MacIntyre has argued that a communitarian ideal, reflecting a fuller conception of the good, would support a much wider range of practical requirements than a welfare liberal ideal. We need to consider, therefore, whether the practical requirements of communitarianism do diverge from the requirements of our other social and political ideals in these respects.

No doubt there is clearly a difference in aspiration between communitarians and welfare liberals. Communitarians hope to enforce a relatively complete conception of the good. By contrast, welfare liberals oppose the enforcement of any complete conception of the good. For example, Rawls contends that his political conception of the good marks the limits of enforceability. To enforce anything more, Rawls claims, would require "the oppressive use of state power."[31] So for Rawls, as for welfare liberals generally, only a partial conception of the good can be justifiably enforced. This permits the adoption of any complete or comprehensive conception of the good that is compatible with the substantive, yet partial, conception of the good that welfare liberals endorse. And it is only in this limited respect that welfare liberals can be said to be neutral with respect to conceptions of the good. Accordingly, it seems far better to avoid this terminology altogether and simply describe the liberal view as requiring the enforcement of a partial rather than a complete conception of the good.[32]

But is there any defense of this welfare liberal commitment to enforcing a partial rather than a complete conception of the good? There is, and the defense is fairly straightforward once it is recognized that a complete conception of the good is not monolithic. For part of such a conception can be maintained, and even caused to flourish, without any enforcement whatsoever. With respect to this part of a conception of the good, therefore, there would be no moral justification for enforcement. Another part of a complete conception of the good is counterproductive to enforce. So here too there would be no moral justification for enforcement.[33] Still another part of a complete conception of the good cannot be reasonably established as good to those against whom it would be enforced. So here too it would seem there would be insufficient moral grounds for enforcing this part of a complete conception of the good. For how could we be morally justified in enforcing a conception of the good upon those who could reasonably object to it?[34] Consequently, at least with respect to these three parts of a complete conception of the good—that part that can be maintained and even caused to flourish without any enforcement whatsoever, that part that is counterproductive to enforce, and that part that cannot be reasonably established as good to those against whom it would be enforced—enforcement is not morally justified. On this account, only a partial conception of the good can be justifiably enforced.

Further, there is nothing in the previous argument that begs the question against the communitarian view because there is no reason why communitarians should be committed to enforcing a complete conception of the good. In fact, I have just given three very good reasons why communitarians should not be committed to enforcing a complete conception of the good.

At the same time, it should be noted that the conception of the good so far specified and defended by MacIntyre is actually relatively formal when compared with the conceptions developed by rival welfare liberal, libertarian, socialist, feminist, and multicultural theorists. In fact, communitarians, in general, have yet to provide an adequate defense of even those practical requirements they endorse in common with these other social and political ideals, let alone an adequate defense of additional practical requirements.

It would seem, therefore, that once the requirements of communitarianism are sufficiently elaborated and qualified to meet various objections that can be raised against them, there should be no difficulty reconciling them with the requirements of our other social and political ideals. At least, this is the case with the account of communitarianism that has been so far elaborated by contemporary defenders.

LEGITIMATE AUTHORITIES AND THE IDEAL OF THE COMMON GOOD

If communitarianism does not provide any justification for practical requirements extending beyond those justified by welfare liberalism, libertarianism, socialism, and feminism, then communitarians should end up endorsing the same coercive institutions as legitimate authorities as would defenders of these other social and political ideals. It remains to be seen whether multiculturalism will be as accommodating. It also remains to be seen whether in terms of these social and political ideals, there are any existing coercive institutions that turn out to be legitimate authorities.

Notes

1. Alasdair MacIntyre, *After Virtue*, 1st ed. (Notre Dame: University of Notre Dame Press, 1981), 152.
2. *Ibid.*, 175.
3. *Ibid.*, 175.
4. *Ibid.*, 178.
5. *Ibid.*, 186–187.
6. *Ibid.*, 188–204.
7. *Ibid.*, 133–134; 167–168.
8. MacIntyre, 241.
9. *Ibid.*, Chapter 7.
10. *Ibid.*, 229–231.
11. Michael J. Sandel, *Liberalism and the Limits of Justice* (Cambridge: Cambridge University Press, 1982).
12. *Ibid.*, 179.
13. John Rawls, *A Theory of Justice* (Cambridge: Harvard University Press, 1971), 31.
14. *Ibid.*, 560.
15. Sandel, 79.

16. MacIntyre, 208.

17. Of course, I argued in Chapter 3 that libertarians are required to endorse much more.

18. However, as I argued in Chapter 3, the premises of Rawls's welfare liberal theory and Nozick's libertarian theory are not really incommensurable because meeting basic needs is not fundamentally a supererogatory requirement of Nozick's libertarian theory or, for that matter, of any libertarian theory, despite the fact that many libertarians still mistakenly think that it is.

19. Alasdair MacIntyre, *Three Rival Versions of Moral Enquiry* (Notre Dame: University of Notre Dame Press, 1990).

20. Alasdair MacIntyre, "Privatization of the Good," *Review of Politics* (1990).

21. John Rawls, "Justice as Fairness: Political Not Metaphysical," *Philosophy and Public Affairs* (1985), Vol 14, 238–239.

22. It has been suggested to me that Sandel's objection to welfare liberalism could be avoided here simply by claiming that the Kantian injunction never to treat persons simply as a means can be overridden when it conflicts with rights to welfare and equal opportunity. Possibly. But it seems to me that the Kantian injunction expresses such a fundamental moral requirement of respect for each and every moral agent that it cannot be overridden on moral grounds.

23. Robert Nozick, *State Anarchy and Utopia* (New York: Basic Books, 1974), 30–32; 228–229.

24. *Ibid.*, Chapter 5.

25. In Nozick's case, the independents would presumably not be acting wrongfully if they were willing to adequately compensate those affected by the use of their risky procedures.

26. Nancy Davis, "Using Persons and Common Sense," *Ethics* 94 (1984): 394.

27. Rawls, *A Theory of Justice*, 179–183.

28. Michael J. Sandel, "Morality and the Liberal Ideal," *New Republic* (1984): Vol 7, 16–17.

29. John Rawls, "The Priority of Right and Ideas of the Good," *Philosophy and Public Affairs* (1988): Vol 17, 264–276.

30. There is some argument for the rejection of libertarianism in Rawls' "The Basic Structure as Subject," in *Values and Morals*, ed. A. Goldman and J. Kim (Dordrecht: Reidel, 1978), 47–71. But, what the argument ignores is that on the libertarian view *fairness* cannot be interpreted as choice from behind an imaginary view of ignorance.

31. John Rawls, "The Idea of an Overlapping Consensus," *Oxford Journal of Legal Studies* (1987): 4.

32. Similarly, I do not think that the most defensible form of liberalism is appropriately characterized as a view in which "the right is prior to the good" because when this claim is correctly unpacked, it only asserts that a certain partial conception of the good has priority over any complete conception of the good that conflicts with it. However, what the claim incorrectly suggests is that the right has primacy and independence over both partial and complete conceptions of the good. On this point, see also

Will Kymlicka, *Liberalism, Community, and Culture* (Oxford: Oxford University Press, 1989), Chapter 3.

33. Rawls appears to be endorsing a justification of this sort in "The Ideal of an Overlapping Consensus."

34. This line of argument obviously appeals again to the "ought" implies "can" principle.

7

Multiculturalism: The Ideal of Respect for Cultural Diversity

It is difficult for anyone to object to multiculturalism understood as the ideal of respect for cultural diversity. In this regard, multiculturalism is something like the ideal of respect for other persons. Everyone endorses the ideal. The question is how to interpret it. One possibility is that the ideal should be interpreted so that it leads to moral relativism. Let us consider this possibility.

CULTURAL DIVERSITY AND MORAL RELATIVISM

Moral relativists think that morality is a matter of opinion and that what is right for you may be wrong for me even if we are similarly situated. Moral relativists take their view to be amply supported by the diverse moral views held in different societies as well as by the level of moral disagreement that exists within any given society. In the United States, there is presently radical disagreement over abortion, homosexuality, and defense spending to name but a few issues. Yet, these disagreements seem to pall when the United States is compared with other societies that presently condone infanticide, polygamy, euthanasia, and even cannibalism.

Nevertheless, in order for moral relativists to draw support for their view from this moral diversity, they must be able to show that the same act could be both right and wrong, right for one society, group, or individual and wrong for some other society, group, or individual.[1] Frequently, however, the act that is condemned by one society, group, or individual is not the same act that is sanctioned by another society, group, or individual. For example, the voluntary euthanasia that is sanctioned by Eskimos as a transition to what they take to be a happier existence for their aged members is significantly different from the euthanasia that the AMA opposes.[2] Likewise, when the Nuer gently lay their deformed infants in the river because they believe that such infants are baby hippos accidentally born to humans, their action is significantly different from the infanticide that most people condemn.[3] Even in the case of abortion, what some people judge to be right (permissible) and what other people judge to be wrong (impermissible) would not appear to be the same act because of the different views that people hold with respect to the moral status of the fetus—those opposing abortion usually claiming that the fetus is a full-fledged human person with the same rights as you or I, while those favoring abortion usually denying that the fetus has this status.[4]

Yet even when the same act is being compared, in order for that act to be right for a person to do, it must be possible for that person, following her or his best deliberation, to come to judge the act as right. Acts that are inaccessible to people's best judgment (like avoiding carcinogens in the Middle Ages) are not acts that could be morally right for them to do.[5] Accordingly, when we evaluate people's moral judgments in the context in which they formed them, it will sometimes be the case that we will recognize that they couldn't have arrived at the judgments that we think are morally right. If so, their judgments would not relevantly conflict with our own, even if what they think is right is not what we think is right.

Of course, this is not to suggest that what we think is right for us to do necessarily is right for us to do. After all, we could be mistaken. It is only to suggest that if we are moral agents capable of moral deliberation, any discrepancy between what we think is right for us to do and what is actually right for us to do must be explained in terms of some kind of past or present failure on our part to follow our best deliberation with regard to the opportunities that are available to us.[6] If it is going to make any sense to say that something is right for us to do, knowledge of that fact must somehow be accessible to us, so that any discrepancy between what we think is right for us to do and what is actually right for us to do must somehow be traceable to a failure on our part to deliberate wisely. Consequently, in order for moral relativism to draw support from the existing moral diversity, there must be acts that are sufficiently accessible to people's moral deliberation such that the same act is judged right by some people using their best moral judgment, and judged wrong by other people using their best moral judgment.

But even this is not enough. Moral relativism must also tell us what morality is supposed to be relative to.[7] Is it to be relative to the common beliefs of a society, to those of a smaller group, or to those of just any individual, or could it be relative to any of these? If it could be relative to any of these, any act (for example, contract killing) could be wrong from the point of view of some particular society, right from the point of view of some subgroup of that society (for example, the Mafia), and wrong again from the point of view of some particular member of that society or subgroup. But if this is the case, individuals would not have any reasonable grounds for deciding what they ought to do, all things considered.

Yet, even supposing that some particular reference group could be shown to be preferable (for example, the reference group of one's own society) problems remain. First of all, in deciding what to do, should we simply ask what the members of our appropriate reference group think ought to be done? But if everyone in our reference group did that, we would all be waiting for everyone else to decide, and so no one would decide what ought to be done. Or we might construe moral relativism to be a second-order theory that requires that the members of our appropriate reference group first decide on some other grounds what is right and then take a vote. If a majority or a consensus emerges from such a vote, then that is what is right, all things considered. So interpreted, "moral relativism" would have some merit as a theory of collective decision-making, but it clearly would require some yet-to-be-determined nonrelativist grounds for first-order moral judgments, and so would not essentially be a relativist theory at all.

Second, the very claim that morality should be specified relativistically is not itself a relativistic claim. Rather, it claims to be a truth for all times and places. But how could this be possible? Shouldn't the truth of relativism itself be assertible as a relativistic claim? One might maintain that while moral judgments are relativistic, the thesis of moral relativism is not itself a moral claim, and hence, need not be relativistic. But if truth is not relativistic, why should the good be relativistic?

In sum, moral relativism faces a number of difficulties. First, it is difficult for moral relativists to show that amid the existing moral diversity there are acts that are sufficiently accessible to people's moral deliberation such that the same act is judged right by some and wrong by others when all are following their best moral deliberation. Second, it is difficult for moral relativists to specify the appropriate reference group from which morality is to be determined. Third, even assuming the appropriate reference group can be determined, it is difficult for moral relativists to explain why their theory is not committed to some nonrelativist account of at least first-order moral judgments. Last, it is difficult to explain why moral relativists are committed to a nonrelativist account of truth. Given these difficulties, it would be best not to interpret the ideal of respect for cultural diversity as leading to moral relativism.

BEYOND MORAL RELATIVISM

But how then are we to interpret the ideal of respect for cultural diversity? In the preceding chapters, we have examined five contemporary social and political ideals: a welfare liberal ideal of fairness, a libertarian ideal of liberty, a socialist ideal of equality, a feminist ideal of androgyny, and a communitarian ideal of the common good. It was argued that these five social and political ideals, when correctly understood, all have the same practical requirements, namely, a right to a basic-needs minimum and a right to equal opportunity. These five ideals, as well as their historical antecedents in the works of Plato, Aristotle, Aquinas, Locke, Kant, Hegel, Marx, Wollstonecraft, J. S. Mill, and others, are all thought to be part of the Western philosophical tradition, and so part of Western culture.[8] But Western culture, so understood, is itself multicultural, an amalgamation of many different cultures tracing its origins through the Greeks to the Egyptians and the beginnings of recorded history, and borrowing from many different cultures along the way.[9] So one might think that respect for cultural diversity should come easily to a people, like ourselves, whose own culture is itself the product of many different cultures.

So how should this respect for cultural diversity be manifested? With respect to social and political philosophy, it should be manifested by an openness to consider the merits of the social and political ideals of other cultures, especially non-Western cultures.[10] If a right to a basic-needs minimum and a right to equal opportunity are to be morally defensible, they must be able to survive in a comparative evaluation with other social and political ideals, including non-Western social and political ideals. What are the chances of these rights actually surviving in such a comparative evaluation?

At the moment, the chances seem to be quite good. This is because any morally defensible social and political ideal, whether Western or non-Western, would seemingly have to endorse the "ought" implies "can" principle and its contrapositive, the conflict resolution principle, because these principles are basic to a moral point of view (see Chapter 3). And in virtue of endorsing these principles, any morally defensible social and political ideal would also have to endorse a right to a basic-needs minimum since the "ought" implies "can" principle secures such a right even within the minimal morality of a libertarian political ideal.[11] Further, a morally defensible social and political ideal could not endorse a right to a basic-needs minimum while rejecting a right to equal opportunity because once the moral relevance of distant peoples and future generations is taken into account, the same considerations that support a right to a basic-needs minimum support a right to equal opportunity as well (see Chapters 4 and 5). Thus, it would seem that the only way that morally defensible social and political ideals could significantly differ from our five social and political ideals in their practical requirements is if they were to impose some additional requirements that went beyond these two rights. Yet, given that these two rights lead both to the equality that socialists endorse (see Chapter 4) and to the androgyny that many feminists defend (see Chapter 5), it is difficult to see how a morally defensible social and political ideal could be still more demanding.

AMERICAN INDIAN CULTURE

Nevertheless, it may be that Western social and political ideals are not demanding enough because they have not adequately faced the question of who is to count in ways that other non-Western social and political ideals have done. For example, many, if not all, American Indian tribes regarded animals, plants, and assorted other natural things as persons in their own right with whom it was possible to enter into complex social intercourse requiring mutual respect.[12] The type of respect required is illustrated by the following account of how a Sioux elder wanted his son to hunt the four-leggeds of the forest.

> shoot your four-legged brother in the hind area, slowing it down but not killing it. Then, take the four-legged's head in your hands, and look into his eyes. The eyes are where all the suffering is. Look into your brother's eyes and feel his pain. Then, take your knife and cut the four-legged under his chin, here, on his neck, so that he dies quickly. And as you do, ask your brother, the four-legged, for forgiveness for what you do. Offer also a prayer of thanks to your four-legged kin for offering his body to you just now, when you need food to eat and clothing to wear. And promise the four-legged that you will put yourself back into the earth when you die, to become the nourishment of the earth, and for the sister flowers, and for the brother deer. It is appropriate that you should offer this blessing for the four-legged and, in due time, reciprocate in turn with your body in this way, as the four-legged gives life to you for your survival.[13]

Wooden Leg, a Cheyenne, provides a similar account.

> The old Indian teaching was that it is wrong to tear loose from its place on the earth anything that may be growing there. It may be cut off, but it should not be uprooted. The trees and the grass have spirits. Whenever one of such growths may be destroyed by some good Indian, his act is done in sadness and with a prayer for forgiveness because of necessities.[14]

Moreover, this respect for nonhuman nature shared by American Indians is based on a perceived identity with other living things. According to Luther Standing Bear, a Sioux chief:

> We are the soil and the soil is us. We love the birds and beasts that grew with us on this soil. They drank the same water as we did and breathed the same air. We are all one in nature. Believing so, there was in our hearts a great peace and a welling kindness for all living growing things.[15]

Arguably, it is this respect for nonhuman nature that has enabled American Indians to live in their natural environment with greater harmony than we in Western culture are presently doing.

Is there, then, something that we in Western culture can learn from American Indian culture? At the very least, an appreciation for American Indian culture should lead us to consider whether we have good grounds for failing to constrain our own interests for the sake of nonhuman nature. In Western culture, people tend to think of themselves as radically separate from and superior to nonhuman nature, so as to allow for its domination. To justify this perspective, people in Western culture often appeal to the creation story in the book of *Genesis*, in the Bible. In one version of this story, God tells humans to

> Be fruitful and multiply, and fill the earth and subdue it. Have dominion over the fish of the sea, the birds of the air, cattle, and all the animals that crawl on the earth. (*Genesis* 1:28)

One interpretation of this directive is that humans are required or permitted to dominate nonhuman nature, that is, to use animals and plants for whatever purposes we happen to have, giving no independent weight at all to the interests of animals and plants. They are simply means to our ends.[16] Another interpretation, however, understands dominion, not as domination, but as a caring stewardship toward nonhuman nature, which imposes limits on the ways that we can use animals and plants in pursuit of our own purposes, thereby making it possible for other living things to flourish.[17]

Obviously, this second interpretation accords better with the perspective found in American Indian culture. However, it is the first interpretation that is most widely accepted throughout Western culture. Given these conflicting interpretations of the Genesis story, it is clear that an appeal to the Bible is not going to be decisive in determining how anyone should treat nonhuman nature. Accordingly, we need to determine whether reason alone can provide any compelling grounds for thinking that we are superior to nonhuman nature in ways that would justify our domination of it.

Obviously, the members of species differ in myriad ways, but do these differences provide grounds for thinking that the members of any one species are superior to the members of any other? In particular, do the differences between humans and nonhuman species provide grounds for thinking that humans are superior to the members of other species? Of course, humans have distinctive traits that the members of other species lack, like rationality and moral agency. But the members of nonhuman species also have distinctive traits that humans lack, like the homing ability of pigeons, the speed of the cheetah, and the ruminative ability of sheep and cattle.

Nor will it do to claim that the distinctive traits that humans have are more valuable than the distinctive traits that members of other species possess because there is no nonquestion-begging standpoint from which to justify that claim. From a human standpoint, rationality and moral agency are more valuable than any of the distinctive traits found in nonhuman species, since, as humans, we would not be better off if we were to trade in those traits for the distinctive traits found in nonhuman species. Yet, the same holds true of nonhuman species. Generally, pigeons, cheetahs, sheep, and cattle would not be better off if they were to trade in their distinctive traits for the distinctive traits of other species.[18]

Of course, the members of some species might be better off if they could retain the distinctive traits of their species while acquiring one or another of the distinctive traits possessed by some other species. For example, we humans might be better off if we could retain our distinctive traits while acquiring the ruminative ability of sheep and cattle.[19] But many of the distinctive traits of species cannot be even imaginatively added to the members of other species without substantially altering the original species. For example, in order for the cheetah to acquire the distinctive traits possessed by humans, presumably it would have to be so transformed that its paws became something like hands to accommodate its humanlike mental capabilities, thereby losing its distinctive speed, and ceasing to be a cheetah. So possessing distinctively human traits would not be good for the cheetah.[20] And with the possible exception of our nearest evolutionary relatives, the same holds true for the members of other species: they would not be better off having distinctively human traits. Only in fairy tales and in the world of Disney can the members of nonhuman species enjoy a full array of distinctively human traits. So there would appear to be no nonquestion-begging perspective from which to judge that distinctively human traits are more valuable than the distinctive traits possessed by other species. Judged from a nonquestion-begging perspective, we cannot find any compelling reason for thinking that we are superior to the members of other species in ways that would justify our dominating them.

Nevertheless, a certain degree of preference for members of the human species can still be justified on grounds of defense. Thus, it would be permissible to defend ourselves and other human beings against harmful aggression even when this necessitates killing or harming animals or plants.[21] In addition, preference for members of the human species can also be justified on grounds of preservation. Thus, it would be permissible to meet one's basic needs or the basic needs of other human beings even when they require aggressing against the basic needs of animals and plants. Our survival as individuals and as a species requires that we be permitted to aggress against the basic needs of at least some other living things whenever this is necessary to meet our own basic needs or the basic needs of other human beings.

However, preference for humans can go beyond bounds. And this would be the case whenever humans engage in aggressive actions that sacrifice the basic needs of animals and plants simply to serve the non-basic interests of humans. We can no more consistently reject domination of nature and yet aggress against the basic needs of some animals or plants whenever this serves our own nonbasic or luxury needs than we can consistently reject the domination of other human beings and aggress against the basic needs of other human beings whenever this serves our nonbasic or luxury needs.[22] Consequently, if the rejection of domination of nonhuman nature is to mean anything, it must be the case that the basic needs of the members of nonhuman species are protected against aggressive actions that only serve to meet the nonbasic needs of humans.

So while there are reasonable grounds for a degree of preference for the members of the human species, there are also reasonable grounds for significantly limiting that preference in ways that approximate the limits accepted by American Indians. It follows that those of us within Western culture have an important lesson to learn from American Indian culture. It is that the intrinsic value of nonhuman species places a significant constraint on how we pursue our own interests.

The ideal of respect for cultural diversity requires that we in Western culture be open to consider the merits of the social and political ideals of other cultures, especially non-Western cultures. Sometimes, as in the case of American Indian culture, there will be important lessons to learn. Sometimes we will have good reasons to reject specific elements of other cultures. Yet throughout, our obligation to seriously reflect upon the social and political ideals of other cultures remains.

Will such reflection even lead us to discover conclusive reasons for rejecting the rights to a basic-needs minimum and equal opportunity? Since our justification for social and political ideals is always comparative, we cannot absolutely rule out this possibility. Nevertheless, as our discussion of American Indian culture suggests, the justification for these rights will probably remain. It will simply need to be reinterpreted in various ways, for example, so as to rule out the domination of nonhuman nature.

MULTICULTURALISM AND APPLYING BASIC RIGHTS

Yet even when the rights to a basic-needs minimum and equal opportunity do not need to be reinterpreted in light of non-Western ideals, knowledge of non-Western cultures is still required for the application of these rights. In particular, the application of these rights to distant peoples requires knowledge of the cultures in which the distant peoples live in order to determine what is necessary for a basic-needs minimum and for equal opportunity. Unfortunately, many First World aid programs have been designed without careful consideration of the local cultures, with disastrous results. Probably the most well-known example of the failure to take into account the knowledge available in local cultures is the so-called Green Revolution.[23]

The Green Revolution was initially carried out in northwest Mexico and in the Punjab region of India. It was publicized as a political and technological achievement, unprecedented in human history. It was proclaimed as a strategy for peace through the creation of abundance. In 1970, Norman Borlaug received the Nobel Prize for peace because of his role in the Green Revolution.

The essential ingredient in the Green Revolution was the development of high-yielding seeds. These seeds, initially wheat and later rice, produced their high yield only in conjunction with the intensive application of chemical fertilizers. Native wheat seeds when subjected to intensive applications of chemical fertilizers would respond by producing a larger plant but not more grain. Borlaug's miracle seeds produced a dwarf plant with a higher grain yield. But these miracle seeds not only required the intensive use of chemical fertilizers, they also required more water than indigenous seeds. Unfortunately, when Borlaug's miracle seeds were being advocated for use in Mexico and India, their liabilities compared with the advantages of local alternatives were not well considered.

In 1905, Sir Albert Howard was dispatched to India by the British government to investigate methods of improving Indian agriculture.

He found that their crops were free from pests, and that insecticides and fungicides had no place in their system of agriculture. He wrote:

> I could not do better than watch the operations of these peasants, and acquire their traditional knowledge as rapidly as possible. For the time being, therefore, I regarded them as my professor of agriculture.[24]

Earlier, in 1889, Dr. John Augustus Voeleker in his report to the Royal Agricultural Society of England stated:

> I may be bold to say that it is a much easier task to propose improvements in English agriculture than to make really valuable suggestions for that of India. To take the ordinary acts of husbandry, no where would one find better instances of keeping land scrupulously clean from weeds, of ingenuity in device of water raising appliances, of knowledge of soils and their capacities as well as of the exact time to sow and to reap as one would in Indian agriculture.[25]

However, after World War I, agriculture in India did experience setbacks, some having to do with the decline of export markets and others stemming from partition. In the mid-1960s the World Bank and USAID offered to provide the financial resources to implement the Green Revolution technology that was being pushed by the Ford and Rockefeller foundations. In 1966, Lyndon Johnson refused to commit food aid to India beyond one month in advance until it adopted the Green Revolution as national agricultural policy. So, under pressure, India signed on.

Initially, it appeared that the miracle seeds worked, but soon problems began to emerge. First, without crop rotation, the miracle seeds attracted pests and diseases and, hence, required the widespread use of pesticides and fungicides. Second, in three to five years, the miracle seeds became so pest- and disease-prone that new seeds had to be developed. Third, chemical fertilizers, unlike farmland manure, did not replace all the nutrients that crops were removing from the soil. So in time the soil lost its fertility and yields began to decline. Fourth, the increased water requirements of the miracle seeds led to waterlogging and salinization of the land as well as conflicts over water rights. Fifth, the new technology was not sustainable, dependent as it was on the availability of chemical fertilizers, new strains of seeds, pesticides, and fungicides.

Was there a better alternative? Surely, there was and it could have been found by working with the knowledge available in the local cultures. Before the Green Revolution, there were important research programs in both Mexico and India on a wide variety of seeds traditionally cultivated by peasants. These programs were consciously undermined by the advocates of the Green Revolution. In India, the Cuttack Institute was working on ways to increase yields of rice based on indigenous knowledge and genetic resources. Nevertheless, for political reasons, the Indian minister of agriculture demanded that the Cuttack Institute turn over its rice germ plasm to an institute set up by the Ford and Rockefeller foundations. When the director resisted, he was removed. Another Indian rice institute operating on a small budget had collected over 20,000 indigenous varieties of rice and was working on a high-yield strategy based on tribal knowledge. It was closed down due to pressure from the World Bank because it had reservations about sending its rice germ plasm to the institute set up by the Ford and Rockefeller foundations.

Thus, the failure of the Green Revolution could have been prevented by taking into account the knowledge available in local cultures. Lack of respect for these local cultures was at the heart of the failure of the Green Revolution as a foreign aid program. Clearly, then, the application of rights to a basic-needs minimum and equal opportunity must proceed with adequate knowledge of the cultures in which people live in order to determine what is necessary for a basic-needs minimum and for equal opportunity. This is what the ideal of respect for cultural diversity demands.

MULTICULTURALISM AND THE EDUCATIONAL CANON

Much of the recent discussion of multiculturalism has focused on its application to educational institutions. In this context, it has been argued that the ideal of respect for cultural diversity requires increased enrollment of minority students, increased hiring of minority faculty, and substantial changes in the canon of what should be taught. In the remainder of this chapter, I want to focus on the third implication of the ideal of cultural diversity: the need for substantial changes in the canon of what should be taught—especially as this relates to social and political philosophy.

While virtually all participants in the current debate affirm the ideal of respect for cultural diversity, they draw radically different conclusions from it concerning the canon of works that should be taught. At one extreme, the radical traditionalists want instruction to focus on the greatest works of Western culture, and they would allow only minimal changes in the canon to include works from non-Western cultures.[26] At the other extreme, the radical pluralists seem to want to provide different educational tracts with different educational canons for different cultural groups.[27] In between these two extremes, there is a full range of positions.[28] How should this debate be resolved?

First, a closer examination shows that virtually no one really holds the position of radical pluralism. Critics have associated this view with Molefi Kete Asante who chairs the Afro-American Studies Department at Temple University, but a closer examination of Asante's views shows that he wants a benign form of Afrocentrism integrated into a common curriculum.[29] So the central questions in this debate turn out to be: What should be included in the common curriculum? How much of the classics of Western culture should be left undisturbed in the common curriculum? How much from non-Western cultures should be added to the common curriculum?

Obviously, the answers that you give to these questions depend on how valuable you consider Western culture to be. If Western culture is the source of your oppression, you will probably not think that you have a lot to learn from it. But what if Western culture is in some respects the source of your oppression and in other respects is also a means of your liberation? If that is the case, you will probably not want to discard Western culture in its entirety. You will want to salvage those parts of Western culture that can serve as a means of your liberation. In the area of social and political philosophy, this means that even the oppressed will have good reason to retain those works of Western culture that support the rights to a basic-needs minimum and to equal opportunity, given that the recognition of these rights worldwide and into the future would virtually put an end to their oppression.

Suppose, then, that those works of Western culture that support the rights to a basic-needs minimum and to equal opportunity are retained in the common curriculum. Will there be room left in the educational canon for any other works in social and political philosophy? Could the radical traditionalists be right that even a selection of the greatest works of Western social and political philosophy will just about take up the entire curriculum? Surely, this could not happen. If it did, it would mean that the greatest works in Western social and political philosophy are opposed to the ideal of respect for cultural diversity. This is because the ideal of respect for cultural diversity requires that we in Western culture openly consider the merits of other social and political ideals as well as acquire the knowledge of non-Western cultures necessary for the implementation of basic rights. To carry out these tasks, works of non-Western cultures must be made part of the common curriculum. So unless the greatest works in Western social and political philosophy are opposed to the ideal of respect for cultural diversity, works of non-Western cultures will have to be part of the common curriculum.

Nor is it conceivable that the greatest works of Western social and political philosophy could retain their moral defensibility while rejecting the ideal of respect for cultural diversity. The reason for this is that if the basic rights of Western social and political philosophy are to be morally defensible, they must be able to survive a comparative evaluation with other social and political ideals, including non-Western social and political ideals. So there is no escaping an adequate representation of non-Western social and political philosophy in the common curriculum.

What, then, would a common curriculum that appropriately combines Western and non-Western works in social and political philosophy look like? One of the companion texts to this book, *Social and Political Philosophy: Classical Western Texts in Feminist and Multicultural Perspectives* (Wadsworth, 1994), is actually an attempt to answer this question. In this text, a survey of some of the greatest works of Western social and political philosophy is combined with some of the greatest related works of non-Western social and political philosophy. Some of these non-Western works are chosen because they parallel the views defended in the Western works (for example, Confucius's work parallels that of Plato or Aristotle). But other non-Western works are chosen because they challenge the views defended in the Western works (for example, American Indian works provide an interesting challenge to the Western social contract tradition of Hobbes, Locke, and Rousseau). Obviously, these challenges to Western social and political philosophy could lead to reinterpretations of the Western works just as our examination of American Indian culture led to a reinterpretation of the basic rights defended in this book. In any case, what is clear is that the moral defensibility of Western social and political philosophy depends on the results of just such a comparative evaluation.

In this chapter, we have explored the multicultural ideal of respect for cultural diversity. First, we considered and rejected the possibility that the ideal leads to moral relativism. Second, we considered how the ideal requires an open consideration of the merits of other social and political ideals, especially non-Western social and political ideals. Third, we noted how an open consideration of American Indian culture would lead people in Western culture to reinterpret the basic rights they find morally acceptable. Fourth, we noted that knowledge of the relevant cultures is necessary for the proper implementation of basic rights in those cultures. Fifth, we argued that the canon in Western culture for social and political philosophy must be broadened to include related great works of non-Western culture; otherwise, the moral defensibility of the canon will be placed in jeopardy.

LEGITIMATE AUTHORITIES AND THE IDEAL OF RESPECT FOR CULTURAL DIVERSITY

Since the ideal of respect for cultural diversity is endorsed by all the defenders of our other five social and political ideals, once it becomes clear what its practical requirements are, as I hope it has in this chapter, we should not expect the ideal to support different coercive institutions as legitimate authorities from those supported by our other five ideals. The problem that remains, however, is whether these six social and political ideals support any existing coercive institutions as legitimate authorities in the societies in which we live.

Notes

1. Richard B. Brandt, *Ethical Theory* (Englewood Cliffs, NJ: Prentice Hall, 1959), Chapter 1.

2. Knud Rasmussen, *The People of the Polar North* (London: Kegan Paul, Trench, Trubner & Co. Ltd, 1908), 106 ff. and Peter Freuchen, *Book of the Eskimos* (New York: World Publishing Company, 1961), 193–206. Cf. Hans Reusch, *Top of the World* (New York: Pocket Books, 1951), 123–126.

3. Mary Douglas, *Purity and Danger* (London, Praeger, 1966), 39.

4. It may be possible, however, to show that even those who deny that the fetus is a person should still oppose abortion in a wide range of cases. See my "Abortion and the Rights of Distant Peoples and Future Generations," *The Journal of Philosophy* (1980); *How to Make People Just* (Totowa, NJ: Rowman and Littlefield, 1988); and "Response to Nine Commentators," *The Journal of Social Philosophy* (1991).

5. This is not to deny that it would have been a good thing to avoid carcinogens in the Middle Ages; it is just that without the concept of a carcinogen, there couldn't have been any moral requirement to do so.

6. See the discussion in Chapter 1.

7. See W. T. Stace, *The Concept of Morals* (New York, Macmillan Co., 1937), Chapters 1 and 2.

8. A culture is a set of socially transmitted behavior patterns, arts, beliefs, standards, institutions, and all other products of human work and thought characteristic of a community or population.

9. Great Britain, which in the nineteenth century could be said to be at the very center of European culture, was considered by its Roman conquerors to be at the outer edges of civilization, and something similar can be said about the United States with respect to Western culture in the twentieth century.

10. Is multiculturalism with its openness to consider the different social and political ideals of other cultures a Western ideal? If it is, it surely is not only a Western ideal, since non-Western cultures (for example, American Indian culture) have also manifested a similar openness.

11. It is hard to see how any social and political ideal could impose more minimal moral requirements than a libertarian political ideal without collapsing into egoism, which, by definition, is not a moral perspective since it imposes no constraints at all on self-interest narrowly conceived.

12. Annie Booth and Harvey Jacobs, "Ties That Bind: Native American Beliefs as a Foundation for Environmental Consciousness," *Environmental Ethics* (1990), 27–43; Baird Callicott, *In Defense of the Land Ethic* (Albany, SUNY, 1989), Chapters 10 and 11; and Donald Hughes, "Forest Indians: The Holy Occupation," *Environmental Review* (1977), 1–13.

13. Karen Warren, "The Power and Promise of Ecological Feminism," *Environmental Ethics* (1990), 146.

14. Edward Curtis, *Native American Wisdom* (Philadelphia, Temple University Press, 1993), 87.

15. Luther Standing Bear, *Land of the Spotted Eagle* (Lincoln, 1933), 45.

16. This view is discussed in Lynn White's "The Historical Roots of Our Ecological Crisis," *Science* (1967), 1203–1207.

17. Lloyd Steffen, "In Defense of Dominion," *Environmental Ethics* (1992), 63–80; Eileen Flynn, *Cradled in Human Hands* (Kansas City, Speed and Ward, 1991), Chapter 3; and Robin Attfield, *The Ethics of Environmental Concern* (New York, Columbia University Press, 1983), Chapter 2.

18. Paul Taylor, *Respect for Nature* (Princeton, Princeton University Press, 1987), 129–135 and R. Routley and V. Routley, "Against the Inevitability of Human Chauvinism," in *Ethics and Problems of the 21st Century*, ed. K. E. Goodpaster and K. M. Sayre (Notre Dame, University of Notre Dame Press, 1979).

19. Nonhuman animals might also be better off it they could retain their distinctive traits and acquire one or another of the distinctive traits possessed by other nonhuman animals.

20. This assumes that there is an environmental niche that cheetahs can fill.

21. For our purposes here, I will follow the convention of excluding humans from the class denoted by "animals."

22. Of course, libertarians have claimed that we can recognize that people have equal basic rights while failing to meet, but not aggressing against, the basic needs of other human beings. However, in Chapter 3, it was argued that this claim is mistaken.

23. The following account of the Green Revolution draws on Vandana Shiva, *The Violence of the Green Revolution* (London, Zed Books, 1991) and Francis Moore Lappe and Joseph Collins, *Food First* (Boston, Houghton Mifflen Co., 1977), Chapters 15 and 16.

24. Alfred Howard, *The Agricultural Testament* (London, Oxford University Press, 1940).

25. John Augustus Voeleker, *Report on the Improvement of Indian Agriculture* (London, Eyre and Spothswoode, 1893), 47.

26. See, for example, Allan Bloom, *The Closing of the American Mind* (New York, Simon & Schuster, 1987) and Roger Kimball, *Tenured Radicals* (New York, 1991).

27. Critics usually associate this view with Molefi Kete Asante. See his *Afrocentric Idea* (Philadelphia, Temple University Press, 1987).

28. See, for example, Edward Said, "The Politics of Knowledge," *Raritan* (Summer 1991); Henry Louis Gates, Jr., "Whose Canon Is It Anyway?" *The New York Times Book Review* (February 26, 1989); and Diane Ravitch, "Multiculturalism: E Pluribus Plures," *The American Scholar* (Summer 1990).

29. Molefi Asante, *Afrocentric Idea* (Philadelphia: Temple University Press, 1987).

8

Protest, Civil Disobedience, Revolutionary Action, and the Law

In 1846, Henry David Thoreau was arrested and confined in the county jail in Concord for refusing to pay a poll tax as a protest against the U.S. government's war against Mexico, its support of slavery, and its treatment of Indians. Two years later, Thoreau gave a public lecture in Concord in which he attempted to justify his illegal protest. This lecture published under the title "Civil Disobedience" subsequently influenced both Mohandas Gandhi and Martin Luther King, Jr., in their practice of nonviolent protest. In 1955, more than a century after Thoreau's protest, Rosa Parks was riding home from work on a bus in Montgomery, Alabama. She was sitting in the first seat behind the section reserved for whites. The bus filled. More white passengers boarded and the bus driver, as required by the segregation laws, ordered her to give up her seat to a white man. Quietly, she refused and was arrested. Her action led to the Montgomery bus boycott, organized by Martin Luther King, Jr., which was a dramatic event in the civil rights movement. These actions by Thoreau and Parks are widely regarded to be acts of civil disobedience. Nevertheless, there is considerable debate concerning how to define an act of civil disobedience and when such acts are morally justified.

DEFINING CIVIL DISOBEDIENCE, LEGAL PROTEST, AND REVOLUTIONARY ACTION

One proposed definition defines a civil disobedient act as follows:

1. It is an illegal act.

2. It is an act whose purpose is to draw attention to what is believed to be a breach of a moral principle that is commonly accepted.[1]

However, following the bus boycott in Montgomery, Alabama, the U.S. Supreme Court declared the segregation laws in Alabama and similar laws elsewhere to be unconstitutional. So, with respect to the highest law of the land, Rosa Parks's action, when she performed it, was not illegal as condition (1) of the definition requires. Of course, we can still view her action as illegal, and so as satisfying condition (1) in the sense that she was legally liable for arrest, given that the constitutionality of these segregation laws had yet to be decided.

Condition (2) of the proposed definition attempts to distinguish a civilly disobedient act from a criminally disobedient act, whose purpose is usually immoral and self-interested, and from a revolutionary act, whose purpose, moral or not, is to overthrow the government. But additional restrictions on what counts as civil disobedience have also been proposed. Abe Fortas argued that in order for an act to be civilly disobedient, one must be willing to accept punishment for the act.[2] John Rawls has argued that a civilly disobedient act must be nonviolent.[3] And still others, like Gandhi, have maintained that for an act to be an act of civil disobedience, it must be justified.[4]

Each of these proposed conditions on a definition of civil disobedience, however, seems unnecessarily restrictive. While normally it may be the case that in order for a person's act of civil disobedience to be morally justified, the person must be willing to accept punishment, surely there can be instances where a willingness to accept punishment is not morally required, as, for example, when the punishment is extraordinarily severe, or when the person's imprisonment would seriously undermine the effectiveness of a morally justified protest movement. Similarly, while normally it may be the case that in order for a person's act of civil disobedience to be morally justified, it is necessary for the act to be totally nonviolent, this need not always be the case. For example, one could imagine protesters violently pushing and shoving to gain entrance to a corporation's main offices where they plan to stage a sit-in to protest the corporation's failure to limit and control its industrial polution. It would also be a mistake to define an act of civil disobedience as necessarily morally justified. This definitional move would deprive us of a useful term to cover morally unjustified acts of illegal protest like Lester Maddox's barring African Americans from his restaurant in 1964 in defiance of what were then newly passed integration laws. It would be preferable to be able to describe acts like Maddox's as simply morally unjustified acts of civil disobedience rather than restricting the term *civil disobedience* to cover only morally justified acts of illegal protest.

When "civil disobedience" is used in the way I am arguing it should be used, it does send mixed signals. On the one hand, it characterizes an act as one of *disobedience* rather than *obedience*, and since obedience is usually taken to be the norm, this suggests that there is a presumption that the act is morally wrong—a presumption that must be overcome in order to show that the act is morally right. On the other hand, it also characterizes the act as one of *civil* rather than *criminal* disobedience, and this suggests, given that its intent is not criminal, that the act may well be morally justified. Since, the adjective *civil* has also come to suggest that the intent of the act is not revolutionary either, this too increases the likelihood that the act can be morally justified, given the assumption that revolutionary acts are just harder to morally justify. Used in this way, "civil disobedience" is clearly not morally neutral since it has both positive and negative moral presumptions. Nevertheless, used in this way, the term still leaves open the question of the overall moral justification of the act to which it applies. When used in this way, defining an act as civilly disobedient does not foreclose the question of its moral justification. That question has to be answered on the basis of further evidence.

Moreover, depriving ourselves of a definition of civil disobedience that leaves open the question of moral justification can also have the undesirable consequence of cutting short the process of evaluating particular acts of illegal protest to determine whether such acts are morally justified. Being able to label certain acts of illegal protest as civilly disobedient without yet deciding the question of whether these acts are morally justified, all things considered, can give us more time to deliberate their moral status. Of course, we do have terms like *murder* where the act by definition is morally unjustified. But in this case, we also have the more general term *killing* for which the definitional and justificatory questions have not been completely merged into each other, because despite the presumption that killing is morally wrong, that presumption can be overcome in particular cases. So, in general, in deciding on a definition of civil disobedience, or any other term, it is best not to collapse the definitional and the justificatory questions into each other unless there is some other more general term available with respect to which these questions are not collapsed.[5]

Suppose then on the basis of the foregoing argument, we accept the definition of civil disobedience proposed earlier as an illegal act whose purpose is to draw attention to what is believed to be a breach of a moral principle that is commonly accepted. We next need to reflect upon the relationship between legal protest, civil disobedience, and revolutionary action. Obviously, civil disobedience should not be the first public response to unjust laws. The first public response should be a legal one of normal politics to get the laws repealed or modified by working through ordinary channels within the political system. The second public response, if normal politics fails so as to be reasonably judged ineffective, is to use legal protest to get the unjust laws repealed or modified. Only if both of these responses fail, so as to be reasonably judged ineffective, does civil disobedience emerge as a viable third response. Finally, only when normal politics, legal protest, and civil disobedience have all been sufficiently tried, so as to be reasonably judged ineffective, is revolutionary action a permissible fourth public response, usually undertaken only when there is some probability of success.

ENGAGING IN CIVIL DISOBEDIENCE, LEGAL PROTEST, AND REVOLUTIONARY ACTION

Most philosophical discussions of protest, civil disobedience, and revolution stop right here. Philosophers are happy to debate the question concerning the adequate definition of political terms like "civil disobedience" or "revolutionary action," but then when it comes to the question of the application of these terms to everyday life, most philosophers tend to retreat into their academic ivory towers. In the United States, however, in the early 1960s to the mid-1970s, this was not the case. Philosophers, responding in part to the demands of their students, were not only willing to defend some definition or other of these terms; they were also willing to say that many of the actions taken in the civil rights movement and the anti-Vietnam War movement were morally justified acts of civil disobedience.[6] By contrast, today there is little or no discussion of the possible justification of contemporary acts of civil disobedience or revolutionary action. College moral problems texts nowadays rarely include a section on civil disobedience, let alone one on revolutionary action.[7] Why? Have the days of justified acts of civil disobedience come and gone with the maturing of the civil rights movement and the passing of the Vietnam War? This appears to be what many people think. Even David Powell, a former leader of the militant Weather Underground in the 1960s and early 1970s, seems to agree. In 1994, when he turned himself in after 24 years on the run, he stated, "I am proud to have fought for my country against the criminal government of Richard Nixon. And I am very happy not to be at war with my government now."[8] But, in order for such judgments to be correct, they have to be based on a correct assessment of the level of injustice that exists in contemporary societies and the correctives that are needed to deal with that injustice. It could be that injustice has sufficiently receded in the United States to a level where it can be effectively dealt with and ultimately corrected simply by normal politics, or in difficult cases, by legal protest. But, how can we determine whether this is the case?

Suppose we try to answer this question by using the evaluation of contemporary social and political ideals found in this book. Here we have examined six contemporary social and political ideals: a welfare liberal ideal of fairness, a libertarian ideal of liberty, a socialist ideal of equality, a feminist ideal of androgyny, a communitarian ideal of the common good, and a multicultural ideal of respect for cultural diversity. The main argument has been that these six social and political ideals, when correctly understood, all have the same practical requirements, namely, a right to a basic-needs minimum and a right to equal opportunity, interpreted so as to accord with the ideal of respect for cultural diversity. These rights, it was argued, are applicable to near, distant, and future people, and lead both to the equality that socialists endorse and to the androgyny that many feminists defend. Given the support that this practical reconciliation provides for these rights, when the laws of a society accord with these rights, we definitely should obey them. But what if the laws of a society do not accord with these rights? What if the laws of a society do not guarantee all its citizens a right to a basic-needs minimum and a right to equal opportunity, and make a reasonable effort to extend these rights to distant peoples and future generations, so as to accord with the ideal of respect for cultural diversity? What if a society gives men better opportunities than women, and what if a society is not respectful of cultural differences? At present, all of these injustices can be found in the United States.

Thus, as we noted in our discussion of the libertarian social and political ideal, 32 million Americans live below the official poverty index, and one fifth of American children are growing up in poverty.[9] This extent of poverty in the United States is reflected in the distribution of property since the opportunities people have are frequently a function of the property they control or the property that is controlled by their family and friends. In the United States, 10 percent of families own 57 percent of the total net wealth and 86 percent of total financial assets and 0.5 percent owns 19 percent of the total net worth and 34 percent of total financial assets.[10] In the 1980s in the United States, the average pre-tax income of families in the top 1 percent increased by 77 percent while income to the bottom 20 percent fell by 9 percent.[11] We also noted that 1.2 billion people worldwide are currently living in conditions of absolute poverty, which Robert McNamara has described as "a condition of life so characterized by malnutrition, illiteracy, disease, squalid surroundings, high infant mortality and low life expectancy as to be beneath any reasonable definition of human decency."[12]

Currently, the United States contributes only 0.22 percent of its GNP to relieve absolute poverty in the world. By any estimate, that is not enough (the Netherlands and Norway each contribute 0.7 percent), and the problem has only grown worse over the last ten years.[13] So, in the United States, we have not yet secured a right to a basic-needs minimum for all our citizens, nor have we made a reasonable effort to extend this right to distant peoples, let alone to future generations.

Moreover, we know from our discussion in Chapter 5, that women do not currently enjoy equal opportunity with men. In the United States, 44 percent of women are raped, between 25 to 33 percent of women are battered in their homes by husbands and lovers, 50 percent of women in the workplace say they have been sexually harassed, and 38 percent of little girls are sexually molested inside or outside the family.[14] Women employed full time still earn $.70 for every $1 men earn. In the world at large, women are responsible for 66 percent of all work produced in the world (paid and unpaid), yet they receive only 10 percent of the salaries.[15] Men own 99 percent of all the property in the world, and women only 1 percent. All of this shows that we are as yet far removed from securing equal opportunity between women and men.

What then should be done? Should we simply try to change the law through normal politics? Should we try to change the law through legal protest? Should we engage in civil disobedience? Should we revolt and overthrow the government?

It should be clear that we are not dealing with minor injustices here. Millions of people in the United States are being deprived of an adequate basic-needs minimum and the basic opportunities to develop their abilities, and many of them are children. And the figures worldwide for those living in conditions of absolute poverty are staggering. The figures indicating the lack of equal opportunity currently experienced by women are staggering as well. Surely, normal politics and legal protest should be used to secure these basic rights as far as that is possible, but since these means have already been extensively tried and major injustices persist, is there any reason to limit ourselves to these means alone? Why not, then, engage in civil disobedience or revolutionary action to secure these basic human rights? Is there any reason to think that civil disobedience or revolutionary action would not be morally justified?

It might be argued that since the U.S. Constitution fails to guarantee its citizens a right to equal opportunity and a right to a basic-needs minimum, we should not use civil disobedience or revolutionary action to try to secure these rights. That the U.S. Constitution fails to guarantee rights to equal opportunity and a basic-needs minimum seems clear enough. If we focus, by way of example, on educational opportunity, a majority of the Supreme Court determined, in *San*

Antonio School District v. *Rodriguez* (1973), that there was no constitutional right to education. Likewise, as we noted, in *Wyman* v. *James* (1971), the Supreme Court's decision presupposed that there was no constitutional right to a basic-needs minimum. The only right to a minimum that was recognized by the Court was one that was conditional upon the state or federal government's interest in providing that minimum.

But surely, if rights to a basic-needs minimum and equal opportunity are fundamental requirements of six widely endorsed social and political ideals, as the main argument of this book maintains, these rights must be guaranteed by any constitution that claims to be morally defensible. Since the U.S. Constitution does not guarantee these rights, it is a fundamentally flawed document.

Now it might be objected that this criticism of the U.S. Constitution is inappropriate because it attempts to evaluate the Constitution, which for the most part was written 200 years ago, by appealing to contemporary social and political ideals. But this is to miss the point of the criticism, which is not so much directed at the Constitution as originally written as it is at the Constitution as presently amended and interpreted. For whenever a society's constitution can be seen to be morally defective in the light of its acknowledged ideals, then, it is incumbent upon the members of that society to amend, or at least to reinterpret, their constitution to make up for those deficiencies. If the main argument of this book is right—that when these six contemporary social and political ideals are correctly interpreted, they all require a right to a basic-needs minimum and a right to equal opportunity, interpreted so as to accord with the ideal of respect for cultural diversity—then, the U.S. Constitution will remain a fundamentally flawed document until it too requires these rights.[16]

Yet clearly, few people today endorse civil disobedience and revolutionary action as a means of securing a right to a basic-needs minimum and a right to equal opportunity. Why is that? To answer this question, it is useful to attend to what distinguishes existing injustices from those that were challenged during the anti-Vietnam War movement and the civil rights movement in the United States.

The anti-Vietnam War movement challenged the legality and morality of the U.S. involvement in the war in Southeast Asia. While the most severe harmful effects of this war were suffered by the people of North and South Vietnam, some of its harmful effects were also widely felt by young men of draft age and their families and friends in the United States. The U.S. draft system required a large number of young men, virtually all those who couldn't get a deferment or an exemption, to become part of the war effort, and, for many, this meant risking their lives in Southeast Asia. According to Kim Willenson,

"Clearly the draft, with its assertion of a government right to demand the sacrifice of young lives in a cause that it could not explain, was the yeast that made [the anti-Vietnam War] movement rise."[17] As a consequence, not just poor peasants in North and South Vietnam, but also a large number of politically powerful people in the United States had something to lose from the continuation of the war in Southeast Asia. So, in the case of the Vietnam War, self-interest and morality blended to create a relatively effective opposition to the war that included acts of civil disobedience and some near-revolutionary actions.[18]

By contrast, failure to secure the basic human rights of a basic-needs minimum and equal opportunity has had much less impact on those who have political power in the United States today. The conflict here is basically between the haves and the have-nots, and, in such situations, it is not surprising that the have-nots have not been very politically effective at pressing their case. What the have-nots need in order to be more effective are powerful allies within the current (unjust) power structure, and this is just what they do not have. So while the justice of their cause is no less than the justice of the cause of the anti-Vietnam War movement, the have-nots of today lack the political power to effectively press their case for basic human rights. It is this lack of effective political power that appears to explain people's failure to presently challenge existing injustices with civil disobedience or near-revolutionary actions.

When we look to the U.S. civil rights movement, especially from 1955 to the passing of the Voting Rights Act in 1965, a similar contrast emerges. Unlike the have-nots in the United States and in the world at large today, African Americans at that time were united in solidarity.[19] It was this solidarity that, for example, made the Montgomery bus boycott nearly 100 percent effective, even though it lasted more than a year.[20] Clearly, no comparable solidarity exists today among the have-nots in the United States or the world at large. The have-nots in the United States are too divided by racial, ethnic, religious, and cultural prejudices to present a united challenge to the common injustices they suffer. So again, it is not the justice of the cause, but the comparative lack of effective political power, that distinguishes the current denial of basic human rights from that denial of basic human rights that was challenged in the United States by the civil rights movement from 1955 to 1965.

Without some source of political power upon which to build, people tend not to be motivated to take the personal risk involved in civil disobedience or revolutionary action. So what explains the lack of civil disobedience and revolutionary action with respect to the current injustices is not the seriousness of the injustices themselves, because they are in every way as serious as the injustices protested by the anti-

Vietnam War movement and by the civil rights movement. Rather, it is the lack of sufficient political power to generate the hope of success and to motivate the personal risk required for civil disobedience and revolutionary action. Thus, while people may have a moral right to engage in civil disobedience or revolutionary action, under certain conditions, because of the risks involved, it may be reasonable for them to do so only when there is enough political power to give some hope of success.

There is, however, at least one bright spot with respect to the possibility of correcting existing injustices. It is the potential that currently exists for ridding society of the injustices against women. Since women are found in all economic levels of society, the feminist movement may, more easily, be able to generate the kind of political power necessary to rid society of the lack of equal opportunity for women. It may also happen that in the process of securing justice for women, other forms of justice are secured as well.

Of course, for the most part, the feminist movement has not been characterized by civil disobedience or revolutionary action, unless we count lesbian separatism as a form of revolutionary action, but that may simply have been a tactical error. For example, the Equal Rights Amendment for women may have failed to gain ratification in 1982 because feminists did not go far enough in challenging existing injustices. Some well-chosen civilly disobedient or revolutionary acts may have been just what was needed to turn the tide.[21] This may also be true today with respect to the variety of reforms that are needed to secure equal opportunity for women.[22]

Obviously, the degree to which the feminist movement or any other movement will be able to correct existing injustices remains uncertain. At the moment, however, what is clear is that many have-nots in the United States and the world at large are being denied their basic rights. Under such circumstances, it remains to be determined what it is that is permissible for the have-nots to do.

By now it goes without saying that have-nots in the United States as elsewhere should consider changing or removing existing injustices, first by normal politics, then by legal protest, then by civil disobedience, and only then by revolutionary action. But what if all of these means have been tried and are reasonably judged ineffective, or, alternatively, what if these means are reasonably judged too costly for those whom they are intended to benefit. If either of these conditions obtain, what is permissible for the have-nots to do? Is it permissible for them to engage in private illegal acts to secure those goods and resources to which they are morally entitled? Would such criminally disobedient acts be morally permissible if either of these conditions obtained? Assuming that normal politics, legal protest, civil disobedience, and revolutionary action have all been tried and reasonably judged ineffective or that such means are reasonably judged too costly for those whom they are intended to benefit, then it would seem that criminally disobedient acts would be morally permissible, provided that they are directed at appropriating surplus goods from people who have more than a fair share of opportunities to lead a good life, and at appropriating such goods with a minimum of physical force. Of course, even when criminally disobedient acts are morally permissible, they will normally be engaged in only when they are likely to be successful in securing at least some of those goods and resources to which people are morally entitled.

Thus, suppose, for example, that Gretchen, who is morally entitled to a $7,000 income, receives only a $4,000 income through legal channels. Suppose, further, that every means of correcting this injustice, save criminal disobedience, has been tried so as to be reasonably judged ineffective or using such means is reasonably judged too personally costly for Gretchen. If this is the case, it would be morally permissible for her to be criminally disobedient, provided that her criminal activity is directed at appropriating surplus goods from people who have more than a fair share of opportunities to lead a good life, and at appropriating such goods with a minimum of physical force. Of course, Gretchen will normally engage in such criminal acts only if there is some likelihood that she will be successful at appropriating the $3,000 income to which she has a basic right.

Suppose, however, that Gretchen is caught by the legal authorities. Should they punish her? In a basically just society, the grounds for punishing a person is the judgment that the criminal, unlike the victim of crime, could have been reasonably (that is, morally) expected to act otherwise.[23] But while this comparative opportunity judgment generally holds in a basically just society, it does not hold in the unjust society in which Gretchen lives. She could not be reasonably expected to act differently. In the society in which Gretchen lives (which appears to be strikingly similar to our own), there would be no grounds for punishing Gretchen's criminal activity.

It is important to be very clear about what characterizes cases in which punishing criminal activity would not be morally justified. First, in these cases, other options (for example, normal politics, legal protest, civil disobedience, and revolutionary action) would have to be either ineffective for achieving reasonable progress toward a just society or reasonably judged too costly for those persons they are intended to benefit. Second, in these cases, there would only be minimal violations of the moral rights of others. This means that in these cases the criminal activity would be directed at appropriating surplus goods from people who have more than a fair share of opportunities to lead a good life, and at appropriating such goods with a minimum of physical force. Hence, criminal activity that harms the less advantaged in society would not be morally justified. Nor would it be morally justified to kill or seriously injure the more advantaged, except in self-defense, when attempting to dispossess them of their unjust holdings. But given that all these requirements have been met, it would not only be morally permissible for persons, like Gretchen, to engage in criminally disobedient actions, it would also be morally required for the legal authorities to withhold punishment in such cases. What this means is that for societies, like the United States, that are making little, if any, progress toward correcting basic injustices, although punishment will still be morally justified with regard to most crimes against persons, it will only be morally justified for *some* crimes against property. Happily, for those who dislike this limited moral justification for punishment in societies like the United States, there is an appropriate remedy: Guarantee the basic human rights required by our six contemporary social and political ideals and more punishment for crimes will then be morally justified.

The main practical conclusions of this chapter can be summarized as follows:

WHEN MORALLY PERMISSIBLE AS A
RESPONSE TO BASIC INJUSTICE

1. Normal Politics ⟶ Always.

2. Legal Protest ⟶ When (1) has been tried and reasonably judged ineffective.

3. Civil Disobedience ⟶ When (1) and (2) have been tried and reasonably judged ineffective.

4. Revolutionary Action ⟶ When (1), (2), and (3) have been tried and reasonably judged ineffective.

5. Criminal Disobedience ⟶ When both I and II obtain:

   I: (1), (2), (3), and (4) either have been tried and reasonably judged ineffective or they have been reasonably judged too costly for those whom they are intended to benefit.

   II: The criminal disobedience is directed at appropriating surplus goods from people who have more than a fair share of opportunities to lead a good life, and at appropriating such goods with a minimum of physical force.

WHEN MORALLY PERMISSIBLE ACTIONS ARE PROBABLE AS A RESPONSE TO BASIC INJUSTICE

1. Normal Politics ———————►When there is sufficient political power to provide some promise of success.

2. Legal Protest ———————►When there is sufficient political power to provide some promise of success.

3. Civil Disobedience ———————►When there is sufficient political power to provide some promise of success.

4. Revolutionary Action ———————►When there is sufficient political power to provide some promise of success.

5. Criminal Disobedience ———►When there is sufficient personal power to provide some promise of success.

PUNISHMENT

Should not be withheld ————► When the criminal, unlike the victim of the crime, could have been reasonably expected to act otherwise.

Should be withheld ————► When it is not the case that the criminal, unlike the victim, could have been reasonably expected to act otherwise.

It is interesting to note how the practical conclusions arrived at in this chapter relate to our earlier discussion of the libertarian ideal of liberty in Chapter 3. There it was argued that when we apply the "ought" implies "can" principle and the conflict resolution principle to the conflict of liberties that exists between the rich and the poor, the liberty of the poor not to be interfered with in taking from the surplus possessions of the rich what one requires to satisfy one's basic needs has moral priority over the liberty of the rich not to be interfered with when using their surplus possessions for luxury purposes. It was further argued that to legitimately prevent the poor from choosing when and how to exercise their "negative" liberty, the rich could institute an adequate "positive" liberty or "positive" welfare rights that would take moral precedence over the exercise of a "negative" liberty or a "negative" welfare right. Of course, the underlying assumption of this whole discussion is that the rich and the poor would do what is reasonably determined to be morally right within a libertarian framework.

But what if the rich refuse to do what is reasonably determined to be morally right? Specifically, what if the rich refuse to recognize the welfare rights of the poor or recognize only inadequate welfare rights, as in the United States today? What then can the poor legitimately do? It is here that this chapter's discussion of the moral appropriateness of normal politics, legal protest, civil disobedience, revolutionary action, and criminal disobedience becomes relevant in deciding what we should be doing in the unjust world in which we live.

We have noted that many people live in societies where the basic human rights required by our six contemporary social and political ideals are not guaranteed, yet where very little civil disobedience or revolutionary action takes place. In this chapter, I have tried to explain this absence of civil disobedience and revolutionary action in a way that provides no justification at all for the practices of these unjust societies. The absence of civil disobedience and revolutionary action is simply due to the lack of sufficient political power to inspire some hope of success. In these circumstances, civil disobedience and revolutionary actions are still morally permissible, but they are unlikely to take place because there is little likelihood that they will be successful. I have also argued that in such societies where basic human rights have been denied, certain criminally disobedient acts thereby become morally permissible, and existing legal authorities have no right to punish them. Rather than punish, the appropriate corrective in such cases is to make the changes required to guarantee just those basic human rights that have been denied.

Notes

1. This definition is close to the one proposed by Jeffrie Murphy in *Civil Disobedience and Violence* (Belmont, CA: Wadsworth, 1971), although it still differs from Murphy's in certain respects.

2. Abe Fortas, *Concerning Dissent and Civil Disobedience* (New York, World Publishing Co., 1968).

3. John Rawls, *A Theory of Justice* (Cambridge, Harvard University Press,

1971): 363–364.

4. Mohandas Gandhi, *Non-Violent Resistance* (New York, Oxford University Press, 1964), 3.

5. It might be objected here that we do have a more general term, *illegal protest,* for which the definitional and justificatory questions have not been merged. It is true that while this term carries a presumption that the protest, because illegal, is morally wrong, this presumption can be overcome by further evidence. So the term does leave the justificatory question open. However, "illegal protest" does not have the additional advantage of sending mixed signals that "civil disobedience" has, when it is used in the way I am proposing that we use it.

6. See, for example, Jeffrie Murphy, "The Vietnam War and the Right of Resistance," in *Civil Disobedience and Violence.*

7. Consider, for example, the four editions of my moral problems text *Morality in Practice* from 1984 to the present.

8. *New York Times* (January 7, 1994).

9. Alan Durning, "Life on the Brink," *World Watch* 3, no. 2 (1990), 29.

10. Federal Reserve Board, "Financial Characteristics of High-Income Families," *Federal Reserve Bulletin* (Washington, D.C., December 1986), 164–171. Richard Parker, *The Myth of the Middle Class* (New York: Harper & Row, 1972), 212.

11. *New York Times* (March 5, 1992).

12. See Durning, 24; Peter Singer, "The Famine Relief Argument," in *Morality in Practice*, 4th ed., ed. James P. Sterba (Belmont, CA: Wadsworth, 1993).

13. *Ibid.*

14. Catherine MacKinnon, *Feminism Unmodified* (Cambridge: Harvard University Press, 1987).

15. Report on the World Conference of the United Nations Decade for Women, Copenhagen, 14–30 July 1981.

16. For further argument, see James P. Sterba, "The Constitution: A Fundamentally Flawed Document," and "A Brief Reply to Three Commentators," in *Philosophical Reflections on the United States Constitution,* ed. Christopher Gray (Lewiston, Mellon Press, 1989) .

17. Kim Willenson, *The Bad War* (New York, 1987), 250.

18. See *An American Ordeal: The Antiwar Movement of the Vietnam Era* (Syracuse, 1990).

19. For the importance of solidarity in the civil rights movement, see Aldon Morris, *The Origins of the Civil Rights Movement* (New York, 1984); Doug McAdam, *Political Process and the Development of Black Insurgency* (Chicago, 1982); and Richard King, *Civil Rights and the Idea of Freedom* (Oxford, Oxford University Press, 1992).

20. For an account of the boycott, see Rhoda Lois Blumberg, *Civil Rights* (Boston, 1984), Chapter 3.

21. For a discussion of this issue, see Jane Mansbridge, *Why We Lost the ERA* (Chicago, University of Chicago Press, 1986), Chapter 10.

22. See Chapter 5.

23. James P. Sterba, "A Rational Choice Theory of Punishment,"

BIBLIOGRAPHY

Ackerman, Bruce A. *Social Justice in the Liberal State*. New Haven: Yale University Press, 1980.

Allgeier, Elizabeth, and Naomi McCormick. *Changing Boundaries*. Washington, D.C.: Institute for Policy Studies, 1983.

Aristotle. *Nicomachean Ethics*. Translated by Martin Ostwald. Indianapolis: Bobbs-Merrill, 1962.

Arthur, John, and William Shaw. *Social and Political Philosophy*. Englewood Cliffs, NJ: Prentice Hall, 1992.

Asante, Molefi Kete. "Multiculturalism: An Exchange." *The American Scholar* (Spring 1991).

Baier, Annette. "What Do Women Want in a Moral Theory?" *Nous* 19 (1985).

———. "Trust and Antitrust." *Ethics* 97 (1986).

Barry, Brian. *The Liberal Theory of Justice*. London: Oxford University Press, 1973.

Bay, Christian. *Strategies of Political Emancipation*. Notre Dame: University of Notre Dame Press, 1981.

Bellah, Robert, et al. *Habits of the Heart*. Berkeley: University of California Press, 1985.

Berubé, Michael. "Public Image Limited: Political Correctness and the Media's Big Lie." *The Village Voice*, June 18, 1991.

Bishop, Sharon, and Marjorie Weinzweig, eds. *Philosophy and Women*. Belmont, CA: Wadsworth, 1979.

Bowles, Samuel, and Herbert Gentis. *Schooling in Capitalist America*. New York: Basic Books, 1976.

Brown, Alan. *Modern Political Philosophy*. Harmondsworth, England: Penguin Books, 1986.

Buchanan, Allen. *Marx and Justice: The Radical Critique of Liberalism*. Totowa, NJ: Rowman & Allanheld, 1982.

Crocker, Lawrence. "Equality, Solidarity and Rawls's Maximin." *Philosophy and Public Affairs* 6 (1977).

Daly, Mary. "The Qualitative Leap Beyond Patriarchial Religion." *Quest* 1 (Spring 1975).

Daniels, Norman. "Equal Liberty and Unequal Worth of Liberty." In *Reading Rawls*, ed. Norman Daniels. New York: Basic Books, 1975.

Diamond, Irene. *Families, Politics, and Public Policy*. New York: Longman, 1983.

Donagan, Alan. *The Theory of Morality*. Chicago: University of Chicago Press, 1977.

Doppelt, Gerald. "Rawls's System of Justice: A Critique from the Left." *Nous* 15 (1981).

Downing, Lyle, and Robert Thigpen. "After Telos: The Implications of MacIntyre's Attempt to Restore the Concept in *After Virtue*." *Social Theory and Practice* 10 (1984).

D'Souza, Dinesh, and Robert MacNeil. "The Big Chill? Interview with Dinesh D'Souza." MacNeil/Lehrer Productions, 1991.

Dworkin, Andrea. *Women Hating*. New York: E. P. Dutton, 1974.

Dworkin, Ronald. "The Original Position." *University of Chicago Law Review* 40 (1974).

———. "What Is Equality? Parts I and II." *Philosophy and Public Affairs* 10 (1981).

———. *A Matter of Principle*. Cambridge: Harvard University Press, 1985.

Eisenstein, Zillah. *Feminism and Sexual Equality*. New York: Monthly Review Press, 1984.

Elshtain, Jean Bethke. "Against Androgyny." *Telos* 47 (1981).

Ferguson, Ann. "Androgyny as an Ideal for Human Development." In *Feminism and Philosophy*, ed. Mary Vetterling-Braggin, Frederick Elliston, and Jan English. Totowa, NJ: Rowman & Allanheld, 1977. Reprinted in 1985.

Fernández, Enrique. "P. C. Rider." *The Village Voice*, June 18, 1991.

Finnis, John. *Natural Law and Natural Rights*. Oxford: Clarendon Press, 1980.

———. *Fundamentals of Ethics*. Washington, D.C.: Georgetown University Press, 1983.

Fish, Stanley. "There's No Such Thing as Free Speech and It's a Good Thing, Too." *Boston Review* (February 1992).

Fisk, Milton. "History and Reason in Rawls's Moral Theory." In *Reading Rawls*, ed. Norman Daniels. New York: Basic Books, 1975.

———. *Ethics and Society*. New York: New York University Press, 1980.

Fowler, Mark. "Self Ownership, Mutual Aid, and Mutual Respect: Some Counterexamples to Nozick's Libertarianism." *Social Theory and Practice* 9 (1980).

Frankena, William. "MacIntyre and Modern Morality." *Ethics* 94 (1983).

Freeman, Jo. *Women: A Feminist Perspective*, 4th ed. Palo Alto, CA: Mayfield Publishing Co., 1989.

Friedan, Betty. *The Feminine Mystique*. New York: W. W. Norton & Co., 1963.

Friedman, David. *The Machinery of Freedom*, 2nd ed. LaSalle, IL: Open Court, 1989.

Friedman, Milton. *Capitalism and Freedom*. Chicago: University of Chicago Press, 1962.

Frye, Marilyn. *The Politics of Reality*. New York: The Crossing Press, 1983.

Galston, William A. *Justice and the Human Good*. Chicago: University of Chicago Press, 1980.

Gates, Henry Louis, Jr. "Whose Canon Is It, Anyway?" *The New York Times Book Review* (February 26, 1989).

Gauthier, David. *Morals by Agreement*. Oxford: Oxford University Press, 1986.

Gordon, Ted, and Wahneema Lubiano. "The Statement of the Black Faculty Caucus." *The Daily Texan*. May 3, 1990.

Gould, Carol C. *Marx's Social Ontology*. Cambridge: MIT Press, 1978.

Gould, Carol C., and Marx W. Wartofsky, eds. *Women and Philosophy: Toward a Theory of Liberation*. New York: G. P. Putnam's Sons.

Gutman, Amy. *Liberal Equality*. Cambridge: Cambridge University Press, 1980.

Harrington, Michael. *Socialism Past and Future*. New York: Arcade Publishing, 1989.

Harsanyi, John C. "Can the Maximin Principle Serve as a Basis for Morality?" *American Political Science Review* 69 (1975).

———. *Essays on Ethics, Social Behavior, and Scientific Explanation*. Dordrecht, Holland: Reidel Publishing Co., 1976.

Hartmann, Heidi. "The Unhappy Marriage of Marxism and Feminism." In *Women and Revolution*, ed. Linda Sargent. Boston: South End Press, 1981.

Hayek, F. A. *The Constitution of Liberty*. Chicago: University of Chicago Press, 1960.

Heilbroner, Robert L. *Marxism, For and Against*. New York: W. W. Norton & Co., 1980.

Held, Virginia. *Rights and Goods*. New York: Free Press, 1984.

Hentoff, Nat. "'Speech Codes' on the Campus and Problems of Free Speech." *Dissent* (Fall 1991).

Hospers, John. *Libertarianism*. Los Angeles: Nash Publishing Co., 1971.

Howe, Irving. "The Value of the Canon." *The New Republic* (1991).

Hudson, Stephen D. "Taking Virtue Seriously." *Australasian Journal of Philosophy* 59 (1981).

Irving, John. *The World According to Garp*. New York: Dutton, 1978.

Jagger, Alison M. *Feminist Politics and Human Nature*. Totowa, NJ: Rowman & Allanheld, 1983.

Jagger, Alison M., and Paula Rothenburg Struhl. *Feminist Frameworks*, 2d ed. New York: McGraw-Hill, 1984.

Kimball, Roger. "The Periphery v. the Center: The MLA in Chicago." *The New Criterion* (February 1991).

Kontos, Alkis, ed. *Powers, Possessions, and Freedom*. Toronto: University of Toronto Press, 1979.

Kourany, Janet, James Sterba, and Rosemarie Tong. *Feminist Frameworks*. Englewood Cliffs, NJ: Prentice Hall, 1992.

Kramer, Hilton. "The Prospect Before Us." *The New Criterion* (September 1990).

Larrabee, Mary Jeanne. "Feminism and Parental Roles: Possibilities for Change." *Journal of Social Philosophy* 14 (1983).

Levine, Andrew. *Liberal Democracy: A Critique of Its Theory*. New York: Columbia University Press, 1981.

Lowden, Robert B. "On Some Vices of Virtue Ethics." *American Philosophical Quarterly* 21 (1984).

Lukes, Steven. "Socialism and Equality," in *Justice: Alternative Political Perspectives*, ed. James P. Sterba. Belmont, CA: Wadsworth, 1980.

Machan, Tibor. *Human Rights and Human Liberties*. Chicago: Nelson-Hall, 1975.

———. *Individuals and Their Rights*. LaSalle, IL: Open Court, 1989.

MacIntyre, Alasdair. *After Virtue*. Notre Dame: University of Notre Dame Press, 1981.

———. *Whose Justice? Which Rationality?* Notre Dame: University of Notre Dame Press, 1988.

Mack, Eric. "Liberty and Justice." *In Justice and Economic Distribution*, ed. John Arthur and William Shaw. Englewood Cliffs, NJ: Prentice Hall, 1977.

Macpherson, C. B. "Rawls's Models of Man and Society." *Philosophy of the Social Sciences* 3 (1973a).

———. *Democratic Theory*. Oxford: Clarendon Press, 1973b.

———. *The Life and Times of Liberal Democracy*. Oxford: Oxford University Press, 1977.

———. *Property*. Toronto: University of Toronto Press, 1978.

———. *The Rise and Fall of Economic Justice and Other Essays*. London: Oxford University Press, 1985.

McInery, Ralph. *Ethica Thomistica*. Washington, D.C.: Catholic University of America Press, 1982.

Mill, John Stuart. *On Liberty*. Indianapolis: Bobbs-Merrill Co., 1956.

Miller, Richard W. "Rawls and Marxism." *Philosophy and Public Affairs* 3 (1974).

———. "Rawls, Risk, and Utilitarianism." *Philosophical Studies* 28 (1975).

Morgan, Kathryn Pauly. "Androgyny: A Conceptual Critique." *Social Theory and Practice* 8 (1982).

Mueller, Dennis C., Robert Tottison, and Thomas Willette. "The Utilitarian Contract: A Generalization of Rawls's Theory of Justice." *Theory and Decision* 21 (1974).

Narveson, Jan. "Rawls and Utilitarianism." In *The Limits of Utilitarianism*, ed. Harlan Miller and William Williams. Minneapolis: University of Minnesota Press, 1982.

Nell, Edward, and Onora O'Neill. "Justice under Socialism," in *Justice: Alternative Political Perspectives*, ed. James P. Sterba. Belmont, CA: Wadsworth, 1980.

Nielson, Kai. *Equality and Liberty*. Totowa, NJ: Rowman & Littlefield, 1985.

Nielson, Kai, and Steven C. Pattin. *Marx and Morality*. Guelph, Ontario: Canadian Association in Publishing in Philosophy, 1981.

Nozick, Robert. *Anarchy, State, and Utopia*. New York: Basic Books, 1974.

Okin, Susan. *Justice, Gender and the Family*. New York: Basic Books, 1989.

Oldenquist, Andrew. *The Non-Suicidal Society*. Bloomington: Indiana University Press, 1986.

Pateman, Carole. *The Sexual Contract*. Stanford: Stanford University Press, 1988.

Perry, Richard, and Patricia Williams. "Freedom of Hate Speech," *Tikkun* 6, no. 4.

Pielke, Robert G. "Are Androgyny and Sexuality Compatible?" In *"Femininity," "Masculinity," and "Androgyny,"* ed. Mary Vetterling-Braggin. Totowa, NJ: Rowman & Allanheld, 1982.

Pincoffs, Edmund. *Quandaries and Virtues*. Lawrence: University of Kansas Press, 1986.

Plato. *The Republic*. Translated by Francis Cornford. New York: Oxford University Press, 1945.

Pollitt, Katha. "Why Do We Read?" *The Nation* (September 23, 1991).

Ravitch, Diane. "Multiculturalism: E Pluribus Plures." *The American Scholar* (Summer 1990).

Rawls, John. *A Theory of Justice*. Cambridge: Harvard University Press, 1971.

————. "Justice as Fairness: Political Not Metaphysical." *Philosophy and Public Affairs* 14 (1985).

———— "The Idea of an Overlapping Consensus." *Oxford Journal of Legal Studies* 7 (1987).

Raymond, Janice. "The Illusion of Androgyny." *Quest* 2 (1975).

Richards, David A. *A Theory of Reasons for Action*. Oxford: Oxford University Press, 1971.

Rothbard, Murray. *For a New Liberty*. New York: Collier Books, 1978.

————. *The Ethics of Liberty*. Atlantic Highlands, NJ: Humanities Press, 1982.

Rothenberg, Paula. "Critics of Attempts to Democratize the Curriculum Are Waging a Campaign to Misrepresent the Work of Responsible Professors." *The Chronicle of Higher Education* (April 10, 1991), B1 and B3.

Rothman, Barbara Katz. "How Science Is Redefining Parenthood." *Ms.* (August 1982).

Said, Edward W. "The Politics of Knowledge," *Raritan* XI, no. 1 (Summer 1991).

Sandel, Michael J. *Liberalism and the Limits of Justice*. Cambridge: Cambridge University Press, 1982.

Schaefer, David Lewis. *Justice or Tyranny*. New York: Kennikat Press, 1979.

Scheewind, J. B. "Virtue, Narrative, and Community." *The Journal of Philosophy* 79 (1982b).

Schweichkart, David. "Should Rawls Be a Socialist?" *Social Theory and Practice* 4 (1978).

————. *Capitalism or Worker Control?* New York: Praeger Publishers, 1980.

Searle, John. "The Storm over the University," *The New York Review of Books* (December 6, 1990).

Shue, Henry. *Basic Rights. Princeton*: Princeton University Press, 1980.

Singer, Peter. *Practical Ethics.* Cambridge: Cambridge University Press, 1979.

Smart, J. C. "Utilitarianism and Justice." *Journal of Chinese Philosophy* 5 (1978).

Smart, J. C., and Bernard Williams. *Utilitarianism: For and Against.* Cambridge: Cambridge University Press, 1973.

Steinem, Gloria. "What It Would Be Like If Women Win." *Time* (August 31, 1970).

Steiner, Hillel. "The Natural Right to the Means of Production." *Philosophical Quarterly* (1977b).

————. "Slavery, Socialism and Private Property." *Nomos XXII: Property*, ed. J. Roland Pennock and John W. Chapman. New York: New York University Press, 1980.

Sterba, James P. *How to Make People Just.* Totowa, NJ: Rowman & Littlefield, 1988.

————. *Justice: Alternative Political Perspectives.* 2nd ed. Belmont, CA: Wadsworth, 1992.

Sterba, James P., and Douglas Rasmussen. *The Catholic Bishops and the Economy: A Debate.* London: Transaction Books, 1987.

Stimpson, Catharine R. "On Differences: Modern Language Association Presidential Address 1990." *PMLA* 106 (1991).

Stretton, Hugh. *Capitalism, Socialism, and the Environment.* Cambridge: Cambridge University Press, 1976.

Timmons, William. *Public Ethics and Issues.* Belmont, CA: Wadsworth, 1990.

Tong, Rosemarie. *Feminist Thought.* Boulder, CO: Westview Press, 1989.

Trebilcot, Joyce, ed. "Two Forms of Androgynism." Reprinted in *Feminism and Philosophy*, ed. Mary Vetterling-Braggin, Frederick Elliston, and Jane English. Totowa, NJ: Rowman & Allanheld, 1977.

————. *Mothering: Essays in Feminist Theory.* Totowa, NJ: Rowman & Allanheld, 1984.

U.S. Commission on Civil Rights. *Statement on the Equal Rights Amendment.* Washington, D.C.: U.S. Government Printing Office, 1978.

Wachbroit, Robert. "A Genealogy of Virtues." *Yale Law Journal* 92 (1983).

Wallace, James. *Virtues and Vices.* Ithaca, NY: Cornell University Press, 1978.

Walzer, Michael. *Spheres of Justice.* New York: Basic Books, 1983.

Warren, Mary Anne. "Is Androgyny the Answer to Sexual Stereotyping?" in *"Femininity," "Masculinity," and "Androgyny,"* ed. Mary Vetterling-Braggin. Totowa, NJ: Littlefield & Allanheld, 1982.

West, Cornel. "Diverse New World," *Democratic Left*, XIX, no. 4 (July/August 1991).

Will, George F. "Radical English." Washington Post Writers Group, 1991.

Williams, Bernard. "A Critique of Utilitarianism," in *Utilitarianism: For and Against*, ed. Bernard Williams and J. J. G. Smart. Cambridge: Cambridge University Press, 1973.

Wolgast, Elizabeth. *Equality and the Rights of Women*. Ithaca, NY: Cornell University Press, 1980.

Women's Economic Agenda Working Group. *Toward Economic Justice for Women*. Washington, D.C.: Institute for Policy Studies, 1985.

Young, Iris. "Humanism, Gynocentrism, and Feminist Politics." *Women's Studies International Forum* 8, no. 3 (1985).

———. *Justice and the Politics of Difference*. Princeton: Princeton University Press, 1990.

INDEX

affirmative action, 70
American Indian, 97–98, 101
anarchism, 7–8
animal rights, *See* nonhuman nature
anti-Vietnam War movement, 115, 118–120
Aristotle, 100, 109
Aristotelian moral theory, 82–84, 86–87, 100
Asante, Molefi Kete, 108
authority, *See* legitimate authorities

basic needs, 15–19, 21, 23–25, 100–105
    of animals, 104
    definition of, 15
    lacking sufficient opportunities and resources to satisfy, 42–43
    nutritional, 18, 58
    related to conflit between rich and poor, 32–45
    related to conflict with nonhumans, 104–5
    related to distant peoples and future generations, 17–19
    universal, 53–55
    variation in the costs of satisfying, 16–17
Bay, Christian, 53
Bergland, Bob, 17
Berlin, Isaiah, 46n.2
Borlaug, Norman, 105

capitalism
    capitalist class, 22–24
    capitalist exploitation, 23–24, 61
    capitalist society, 48, 65
China, 18
Christoforou v. *Ryder Truck Rental*, 74
civil disobediance, 112–115
    conditions on, 113–114
    definition of, 113
    engaging in, 115
civil rights movement, 115, 118–120, 125n.19
Clark, Barry, 59
    coercive institutions, 1–2, 6, 8, 9n.1, 25, 45, 61, 77, 94, 110
comparable worth, 70, 77, 79n.17, 79n.20, 79n.25
compromise view, 14–15, 26n.7
conflict resolution principle, 35–37, 100, 123
Confucius, 109
coordination problem, 39, 47n.15
criminally disobediant acts, 114, 120–124
Cuttack Institute, 107

Davis, Nancy, 90–91
day care, 67
democratic control
    of the flow of investment, 59–60
    of the workplace, 49, 52–53, 59
dilemmas
    moral, 4–5
distant peoples and future generations, 12, 15, 17–18, 56–58, 60–61
duties, 12
Dworkin, Ronald, 19, 92